Dallas and the Spitfire

AN OLD CAR, AN EX-CON, AND AN UNLIKELY FRIENDSHIP

TED KLUCK & DALLAS JAHNCKE

BETHANYHOUSE
a division of Baker Publishing Group
Minneapolis, Minnesota

© 2012 by Ted Kluck and Dallas Jahncke

Published by Bethany House Publishers
11400 Hampshire Avenue South
Bloomington, Minnesota 55438
www.bethanyhouse.com

Bethany House Publishers is a division of
Baker Publishing Group, Grand Rapids, Michigan

Printed in the United States of America

Library of Congress Cataloging-in-Publication Data
Kluck, Ted.
    Dallas and the Spitfire : an old car, an ex-con, and an unlikely friendship / Ted Kluck and Dallas Jahncke.
        p.   cm.
    Summary: "Memoir about a suburban dad mentoring a twenty-something former drug addict/convict as they restore a classic car together"—Provided by publisher.
        ISBN 978-0-7642-0961-1 (pbk. : alk. paper)
        1. Discipling (Christianity) 2. Mentoring—Religious aspects—Christianity. 3. Jahncke, Dallas. 4. Kluck, Ted. I. Jahncke, Dallas. II. Title.
    BV4520.K58 2012
    285.7092′2—dc23   2011045021

All names, dates, and events in this account are factual. However, the names of certain locations have been changed in order to protect their privacy.

The internet addresses, email addresses, and phone numbers in this book are accurate at the time of publication. They are provided as a resource. Baker Publishing Group does not endorse them or vouch for their content or permanence.

Cover design by Lookout Design, Inc.

Authors are represented by Wolgemuth & Associates

12   13   14   15   16   17   18   7   6   5   4   3   2   1

Contents

Contents

Introduction

The Kid Ain't Right

There's a coffee shop in our city called Biggby's. It's the kind of place that always has a fashionable college girl with a pseudo-rebellious nose ring and one or two tattoos working behind the counter. It's the kind of place that always has one or two skinny guys with hip glasses typing on Macs, desperately hoping somebody will ask them what they're working on.[1] It's the kind of place that has Michael Bublé music piped in the background, and where the pseudo-rebellious girl is contractually obligated to make pleasant chitchat with you in a way that makes it seem that even though you know (and she knows) that she's obligated to make the chitchat, she sort of enjoys it. All that to say, it's every coffee shop in every suburban strip mall in every city in America. It's where I'll meet Dallas Jahncke for the first time.

Our church—a smallish[2] Reformed church in East Lansing, Michigan—is big on people meeting with other people. This

---

1. This never happens.
2. When I first started brainstorming this book, and meeting with Dallas, the church was smallish . . . but now the church is well on its way to huge-ish.

is called discipleship, which is a term that has always made me a little uncomfortable, even though I know it's biblical and therefore shouldn't make me uncomfortable. I just don't really feel qualified to disciple anyone. I have lots of friends—I feel qualified to have friends and have relationships with people—but when it comes to the practice of giving spiritual advice, I feel a little lacking. Granted, on paper, I'm different enough from Dallas to be able to give him advice; I've been happily married for thirteen years and have a couple of kids, a house in the suburbs, and semi-gainful employment.[3] But I have bouts of depression, long stretches of spiritual apathy, and a seriously nasty sarcastic streak. And I've had a ridiculously bad year so far. Two thousand ten has seen the dissolution of an international adoption that we'd been working hard on and paying through the nose for, and the falling-through of two business (read: book) deals that seemed like slam dunks. Everything I've touched in 2010 has turned into a huge pile of garbage. Hence my trepidation at "discipling" young Dallas. As much for him as for myself.

Another thing that makes me feel weird about the evangelical "people meeting with people" culture is the idea that when you meet with someone, you can't make a life decision of any kind without running it by them first. The Discipler becomes a de facto Life Coach. And while this "people meeting with people" phenomenon has been mostly good for our church, there are still a lot of college guys walking around who don't have the backbone to have a cup of coffee with a girl without running it by six elders and reading four books by dead puritans first. I think this is ridiculous.

3. Though anyone who has ever worked as a writer knows how precarious and flimsy this statement is. It feels like a miserably hopeless racket sometimes.

All of this is running through my head as I prepare to meet with Dallas. I've heard some things about this kid. I know he lives in the Lansing City Rescue Mission. I know he's been in and out of jail a few times. I know he was a drug addict. And I know I was tabbed for this job because I have experience dealing with rough people, i.e., I watch boxing, have written a book about Mike Tyson,[4] and played semi-pro football with all manner of formerly incarcerated men. I have the bruises and scars to prove it, and I don't so much walk into the coffee shop as painfully shuffle. As any football player knows, this is the chronic pain that comes from being in-season.

I order a tall, skinny decaf mocha from the girl with the quasi-rebellious tattoo.[5] When Dallas enters, he is covered from head to toe in tattoos of his own—and these aren't the kind you get with a friend on spring break after a night of drinking. They're not even the typical "I watch UFC and am a tough-guy-wannabe" tats.[6] And they're definitely not the Christian hipster "Bible verse in Greek" tats. These are the Serious Issues kind of tats.

"I did most of these myself," he explains. His voice is a mixture of mid-South (he spent some time in Tennessee) and Midwest. He's a white guy, probably around five feet eleven, but stocky, around 230 pounds. Apparently, as the story goes, when he first got to the mission he weighed about three hundred pounds and had a long, Jim-the-Anvil-Neidhart[7] goatee

4. Who, himself, wrote the book on being a rough person (see: prison, see: facial tattoos).

5. It's a cross with a little loop on the top part, on the inside of her wrist. I make a mental note to look up the meaning of this when I get home, but I know I won't.

6. See: barbed wire around bicep.

7. This is a reference you'll only get if you watched wrestling in the '80s or early '90s. If you haven't done so already, you should Google-image (verb) Jim "the Anvil" Neidhart.

that stretched down to mid-chest. A real bad-looking dude. Now, he's clean shaven with a face that is sort of cherubic— which is a fancy way of saying it's round and friendly looking. In fact, all of the tattoos look kind of incongruous beneath such a friendly and young-looking face. This kid has lived a lot of life for a twenty-one-year-old.

His knuckles, each bearing a letter, read "Aint Right" (sic). I consider asking him why he didn't devote a whole finger to an apostrophe, but instead ask him the story behind the tats.

"My dad started getting me drunk when I was eight years old," he explains. I try to hide my shock. "And when he would get drunk, he would get violent. . . . He smacked us around quite a bit. And he always used to tell me that I ain't right. So I wrote it on my fingers." Dallas's mother and father are deceased. Both had issues with substance abuse. He has two brothers whom he loves dearly, and whom I can quickly tell is loyal-to-the-grave-to, but both of them are in various stages of the penal system, and both struggle with similar addictions. He is, in terms of practical "making it" purposes, alone in the world. That is, aside from the auspices of the Lansing City Rescue Mission[8] and his friends at University Reformed Church.

His neck reads "No Regrets," though, ironically, he would admit that he has lots of them. "I did this one night after my girlfriend broke up with me," Dallas explains. "I went home and drank an entire bottle of tequila, ripped the mirror off

8. Since 1911, the Mission has existed to meet physical needs to bring those with spiritual needs to Jesus Christ. Their ministries reach out to men, women, and children in the capital area, and they provide food, shelter, and clothing to those who are homeless or low income. Thomas and Emily Dolton founded the Mission as a faith ministry, and it continues to rely solely on the gifts of compassionate individuals, churches, and organizations.

the wall, and tattooed my own neck." I probably couldn't write out the words "no regrets" on a piece of paper, stone sober, as legibly as they're written on Dallas's neck.

Each wrist bears a picture of a razor blade breaking the skin to commemorate his suicide attempts. It was the last of three suicide attempts that landed him in the Lansing City Rescue Mission, a small residential rehab facility in downtown Lansing that sits right next to a piano bar. He lives on the second floor of the Mission, in a barracks-style room with all manner of other Lansing-area homeless guys and drug addicts. The Mission orders his time these days, and he spends it going from AA[9] to CR[10] meetings, Bible studies, and the gym. Before landing in the Mission, Dallas was homeless, often sleeping in tents or barns, and drinking himself to sleep.

"After I attempted suicide the third time, they wouldn't release me from the hospital unless I agreed to go into some kind of residential rehab," he explains. "My caseworker called all over, and the only place that would take me was the Mission." The executive director at the Mission, Mark Criss, made it clear that they were a Christian program and that they would only take men who were willing to live by their standards and at least make an attempt to study the Bible. "My caseworker said, 'That sounds exactly like what he needs.'

"People had tried to share the Gospel with me in prison before," Dallas explains. "But I was never ready for it. I always ignored them because I didn't want to change the life I was living." As Dallas talks, he doesn't act like someone who is excited to be the center of attention. He doesn't find anything

9. Alcoholics Anonymous.
10. Celebrate Recovery.

inherently exciting about his life. He speaks softly, with his head down or his eyes on something else. He seems tired.

Because he had no choice, he began attending Mission Bible studies and found himself moved by the message of the Gospel.

"What I was doing wasn't working," he says.

Dallas cut an imposing figure in the Mission, whose culture is not entirely unlike that of a prison. Fights are frequent. Theological discussions often turn violent, ironically. The longer he'd been there, however, the more likely it was that he could be found sitting in a common area reading Scripture or a book on theology.

"I've read both of your books on the church," he says matter-of-factly. "But I really want to read the book on Tyson." We talk about fighters for a long time. He remembers purchasing some of the Tyson pay-per-views with friends. We both love boxing for its violence and aggression, but also for its respect and self-control.

"I've got some anger issues," he says, in what may be the understatement of the year. He still has outstanding warrants for aggravated assault in the court system, although sitting here today, that's hard to imagine. The man in front of me is gentle, soft-spoken and, well, *new*.

● IN THE WORDS OF DALLAS . . . ●

So I graduated from the Lansing City Rescue Mission transformational program[11] on Thursday, and I'm adjusting to being back in society. Life is a lot different for me now; it seems surreal at

11. This is a one-year drug and alcohol rehabilitation program. There are twelve beds available, and the Mission provides biblical counseling, classes, food, hygiene items, and other necessities at no charge.

times. After having an extreme amount of accountability and little personal authority over my schedule, being able to decide almost completely how I want to spend my time has been a drastic change. When I'm not working, I spend a lot of time walking around aimlessly and hanging out at the library. I have also learned quite a bit about temptation in the last couple of days. It's everywhere.

This is the longest I've been sober since I started using and abusing. I gotta say it feels good to be sober, but it also feels kind of weird. Life is definitely much better now that I'm actually experiencing it with all my senses.

I have had to really rely on God to keep me strong lately. Being in the Mission, I was protected from a lot of things because of the ever-present authority of the Mission. But things are much different now; there is still authority around (I'm in transitional housing), but not like before. It's been a huge test of integrity, but my relationship with God is steadily growing stronger. Every time I'm faced with a temptation or struggle, I am forced to turn to God because I know I don't have the power on my own to make the right decision.

A good friend once gave me the best advice, and oddly enough it was in Scripture form: "Therefore, my brothers, be all the more eager to make your calling and election sure. For if you do these things, you will never fall" (2 Peter 1:10). I received this advice almost a year ago, and it has helped me immensely to become a stronger, God-glorifying man. I'm not perfect, but that Scripture has shown me just how important it is to seek after God and to mortify that old man. It's also a promise from God that He will never abandon me, but I still have to work to live a righteous life.

Critical to this process are all my friends and church family. They've "been there" for me in my times of need, provided me solid biblical advice, and listened when I needed to talk. They have been—and continue to be—better friends than I deserve. I love them. I appreciate their genuine care for me.

Shortly into our latte-sipping session it occurs to me that neither Dallas nor I are really the latte-sipping types. I tell him, offhandedly, that I have a boxing ring in my basement left over from another book project. His eyes light up. "Really?" he asks. Really. And with that, we are waving good-bye to Art School Confidential behind the counter and are soon standing in the ring in the basement. Dallas has the gloves on and I'm wearing target mitts, moving around the ring and teaching him the basics of a difficult sport. Dallas has been in more street fights than he can remember, but he looks awkward and out of place in the ring. He's having the time of his life learning how to throw a jab followed by a left hook, hearing the satisfying *thwack* of a punch well-thrown. "That was sick," he says afterward. *Sick* being a compliment.

Other things that are sick (good): watching fight films in my basement; eating Kristin's (my wife) cooking; hanging out with our family; hip hop;[12] our church; our pastor, Kevin DeYoung.

I find out later that Dallas is a talented artist. He has painted murals in the Mission based on scenes from "Pilgrim's Progress." And he's great at working on cars. We hatch a plan. As we get to know each other, it's clear that we'll need a reason to get together besides just drinking coffee and sharing our feelings. Reading a book together is played—we both read a bunch on our own.

12. We both like Eminem, 50 Cent, and Dr. Dre's *The Chronic*, which may be the greatest hip-hop album ever, top to bottom, even though it's about pot.

"Let's work on a car," I suggest. Again, eyes light up.

"That would be sick," he replies.

I'm terrible at working on cars. In fact, check that, I've never worked on a car. I get nervous at Jiffy Lube when they ask me to pop the hood. I literally have to look around for the latch that does this. That's how not-often I pop the hood, of my own volition. Dallas's dad, in addition to getting him hooked on drugs and alcohol, was also an above-average mechanic, and before his death taught Dallas all he knew. Dallas knows his way around a vehicle, and what's more, he likes doing this stuff.

I've also never had a car that's remotely cool. The Official Car of University Reformed Church is a silver Honda Odyssey minivan with a patina of dried milk and Cheerio residue coating the interior. My own car, a Pontiac Vibe, has the same gross patina. While children are a blessing, there's something patently uncool about being a parent. The stereotype bugs me.

We turn to eBay in our quest for a sick[13] ride. Our plan is to spend less than $2,000 on an old European convertible that we can restore in my garage. Since I'll spend all the money upfront, the car will be mine, but Dallas will be able to use it as often as he likes. The idea of doing this makes me both excited and also sick[14] with anxiety. I can see failure written all over it.

It occurs to me, watching Dallas's baptism in a small Lansing church just days after our first meeting, just how clearly God drew Dallas to himself. On paper this story is impossible.

13. His words.
14. The real sick this time.

But in real life, it's proof that despite its problems, church is good, preaching is important, Scripture has unbelievable transformative power, and—despite the fact that programs like the Lansing City Rescue Mission have unbelievably high failure rates—they work sometimes.[15]

I always cry at adult baptisms. I cried at my own. And it has nothing to do with the drama or lack of drama in a person's testimony. My testimony is delightfully boring. I grew up in a household where both parents loved each other and loved the Lord. It wasn't without issues, but I had parents who I knew had my best interests at heart. I also grew up in a little blue-collar town with lots of Dallases: lots of kids who didn't have it nearly as good as I did.

Our church doesn't have a baptismal, so we had to borrow the church down the street. It's always weird visiting other churches. They all have their own distinctly institutional smells, which is something like hymnal pages/bindings mixed with the remnants of potluck dinners. This one is no different. It's a strange room filled with a strange assortment of people. Our associate pastor is on the piano, leading us through hymns. The seats are filled with a smattering of guys from the Mission, who themselves are in various stages of recovery. Also present are all of the folks in our small group—a theoretical mathematician, a technology guru and his family, Kevin's wife and kids, and us.[16]

After Dallas's testimony, he and Kevin disappear down a tunnel for a minute, and then reappear wearing shorts and

15. Dallas has shared that he feels like "The Great White Hope" at the Mission, because it's so rare that stories turn out as well as his. In fact, he feels a lot of pressure because of this, which is something we'll get into later.

16. As a group, we've decided that in the fall we're going to drive Dallas up north, where he'll be attending a small Baptist Bible college. Since he has no parents, we'll be dropping him off at college. Some of the guys and I are even going to dress "Dad," i.e., plaid pants, etc., in order to make him feel as uncomfortable as possible.

T-shirts. Dallas's shirt is sleeveless, revealing all of his tats. Kevin explains the sacrament to Dallas before dunking him in the baptismal pool. Watching this happen elicits a lot of emotions. It forces me to consider my own salvation—something that, honestly, I take for granted most days. Seeing Dallas's life change, and seeing the church and the Bible through his eyes, has been instructive, to say the least. It's powerful to see the work that Christ does in the life of sinners, of which (like Paul), I am the worst. Romans 3 is one thing when it's espoused from the pulpit for the thousandth time by a preacher;[17] it's another thing to see it standing in front of you in a baptismal pool.

In that moment, I feel blessed beyond words.

I'm also struck by how hard this is going to be. For a recovering addict, each day is not only an exercise in the typical problems of life—things like bills, girls, and work—but also a daily battle to flee temptation and stay sober. The days ahead aren't going to be easy. The thought that discipleship is more than a bi-weekly cup of coffee momentarily freaks me out. So I'm glad we have the car, but I also fear failure—failure to turn it from a heap of metal into something drivable, and also my failure to be a good friend to Dallas, to be what he needs, which is part dad and part brother.

After the baptism, Dallas finds us waiting for him in the lobby. I'm wiping away tears because crying isn't really appropriate for a tough guy writer/baller of my stature. He sees right through it. We embrace.

"For the first time in my life," he says, "I feel like I have a family."

---

17. Reformed preachers seem contractually obligated to exposit the book of Romans, without stopping, for at least a year or two.

1

Loaded Like a Freight Train

I always tell the truth. Even when I lie.

—Tony Montana, *Scarface*

● DAYS OF ADDICTION—BY DALLAS ●

Masochism: pleasure produced by being abused or dominated.
This is how I define my addiction. I knew it was destroying
me, I even knew it was killing me, but I enjoyed it so much
that I never wanted it to end. With every drink, snort, and puff,
I brought myself closer to destruction and death; and yet re-
gardless of my knowing this, the whole time I wanted more—I
needed more. Besides, I could quit whenever I wanted, right?
But the lust of the flesh is never satisfied, so the vicious circle
continued until the game was no longer fun. By then I was too
far gone to help myself. It started out as a packed party, but in
the end I was alone dancing with the devil.

I was eight years old when I first tried drinking and smoking
pot. My mom was dying of cancer and wasn't tuned in to reality

because of the combination of painkillers, chemo, radiation treatments, and the pressure on her brain from the baseball-sized tumor growing within her skull. My dad was always away at work, trying to support us and chip away at the massive debt accumulating from my mom's hospital bills. When he was around, he also chemically numbed himself to escape what was going on. My two brothers and I grew up fast. We had to raise ourselves on our own from an early age, and we didn't always make the best decisions. I found a sweet release from my problems and worries by drinking and drugging. With every hit and drink, my troubles seemed to dissipate; the only thing that was real was the moment I was in and the buzz I was enjoying.

At the age of ten, my mom's inevitable death came, and my world seemed even darker than I thought imaginable. All I wanted to do was escape from the heartache and pain in my life. Suicide seemed like the logical answer to all my problems. My thought process was selfish and twisted: If you don't like life, take yourself out of it. So after a bottle of liquid courage, I tried exactly that. I thought I did my math right: 1 rope + 1 branch + 1 tired and lonely kid = escape from reality. Luckily for me I've never been that great at algebra, because I didn't take into account the x factor. God intervened and the rope broke. Now, if you think about how depressed you have to be to try to commit suicide, think about how you would feel if you tried but couldn't even get that right. Since I couldn't remove myself from reality, I did the next best thing; I completely numbed myself to it.

Fast-forward five years. What started out as a way to escape my problems became a problem in and of itself. The thing about addiction is that the longer you use, the less effect the substance has on you. So I went from a stoner and a drunk to a complete junkie within a few years. The pot and alcohol just wasn't giving me the feeling I needed anymore, so I turned to whatever else I could get my hands on. This created more problems in an already hostile environment. I was always fighting with my dad—and when I say fight, I mean fight: walls were destroyed, knuckles were broken, and there were bruises, blood, and hot tempers. This is the world I lived in. We were so much alike, so stubborn and unwilling to change or show any emotion toward each other except anger. Eventually we both became tired of each other. He wanted me out and I was much too happy to oblige. So at fifteen I became homeless, and oddly enough I felt liberated. I dropped out of school and off the face of the earth.

Michigan winters are brutal if you're living on the streets.[1] I knew I had to get out of the cold or I would be dead soon, so I did what I had to do. I broke into abandoned houses to sleep, and I occasionally stayed with people I got high with. Existing like that gets old real quick. So I made some calls, and before long I was hitchhiking my way to southwest Detroit to stay with some people I barely knew. Life in Detroit is a lot of fun if you're into complete chaos and wondering if you're going to get shot on your way to the liquor store. When you live in an area similar to a war zone, you have two options: be the victim or be the aggressor. I chose to take the world hostage and confiscate everything that I thought should be mine.

I started doing dirt (in thugster terms, dirt is Ebonics lingo for crime and street justice) as soon as I got to Detroit. The people I stayed with gave me the lay of the land, and I hit the ground running like a seasoned vet. I needed to support my habits, and to support habits as bad as mine, I needed money—and lots of it. I robbed houses, stole cars, and mugged people; you name it, I probably did it. I'm not proud of those times, but at the time all I was worried about was myself and getting high. I started running with some really shady and dangerous people in the pursuit of my next high. This is when I made my connection

1. From Ted: They're brutal—physically and emotionally—even if you're not living on the streets.

with the Folk Nation, a street gang that originated in Chicago and has spread its roots of destruction all across the nation. With them I found a new family and a new love: cocaine. I had tried coke before, but I might as well have been snorting baby aspirin compared to this stuff. It was love at first snort. This coke took me higher than I'd ever been before, and I did whatever it took to stay in the embrace of my new lover.

If you have ever romanced coke yourself, you know she's a high-maintenance girl. She demands all your time, money, and attention. I started spiraling out of control, selling coke and doing dirt on the side, but I always seemed to come up short when all was said and done. This is when I broke the number one rule of drug dealing: Never get high on your own supply. Once I crossed that line, I could never go back. I started shorting everybody on the deals I made and ripping people off within the Family (the gang). I might as well have pinned a bull's-eye on my back; before long, even the people closest to me wanted me dead. I knew it was time to leave when the house started getting shot up.

So the people I was staying with and I made our journey to southern Ohio, running away from the madness I helped create. Wilmington was the definition of small-town USA: white picket fences, parades, families with their 2.5 kids . . . It was the American dream in one tightly knit community. I tried to make a new beginning for myself there. I got a legit job cooking at a restaurant and was starting to save money, but demons have a way of following you wherever you go. Who knew there would be so many drugs in such a backwoods town? I noticed there was a lot of traffic coming and going from the house across the street from mine. Curiosity got the best of me, so I introduced myself to the man who happened to be one of the biggest importers of cocaine in the area. It didn't take long before we struck up a business deal, and my infatuation with coke was inflamed again.

I started out as his driver when he made runs to Dayton to re-up, then I moved my way up to becoming a handler, selling to the people he connected me with. He not only sold powder, he also showed me the art of how to cook and sell crack too.

I couldn't resist the urge to try smoking crack. With that first hit I was wired for sound—it was like a train roaring full-speed through the inside of my head. Smoking crack and snorting powder are two completely different types of highs. Crack makes you paranoid and fiendish, searching the carpet for that long-lost rock you think you might have dropped. It definitely wasn't for me. Who knew a junkie could have standards? I preferred the real deal, the high you can only get by snorting some pure, fresh-cut coke. It was a lot cleaner high, but I did indulge in rocks of crack every now and then when things went dry. (Dry: short supply or scarce product.) It didn't take long before I was out of control again, with all the availability of drugs. I stayed high all the time and lost my job, my chances of a fresh start, and, most of all, my sanity. I was back to the old way of doing things. Out of money? That's okay, there are plenty of un-suspecting people to rob in small-town USA.

But there was a major difference that I didn't factor in. This wasn't Detroit, and cops in Wilmington didn't take too kindly to people like me disturbing the American dream. Eventually the combination of rage and coke altered my future forever. When I wasn't out doing dirt, I would try to find odd jobs to make money. One of the jobs I managed to secure involved clean-ing out a condemned house to prepare it for demolition. When the week ended, I went to the house of the man who hired me to collect my pay, but instead of handing me money, the man just laughed and slammed the door in my face. Needless to say, I was furious. I stayed up all night getting high and, as the night went on, my blood started to boil with rage. Before long I snapped, losing any amount of common sense that I had left.

23

I went to the guy's house and kicked in his front door, and after that everything is a blur. I proceeded to beat the guy up as his family begged me to stop, and then I stole everything in sight that I could carry.

I went home knowing I was in trouble. It didn't take long for word to get out about what happened, and soon the cops were looking for me. I knew I couldn't run forever, so I manned up and turned myself in. After a plea of no-contest, my rap sheet now included five felonies and three misdemeanors. I spent three months in county jail during my trial, but since I was one month shy of my seventeenth birthday, after I was convicted I was sent to juvenile prison. I spent one month in intake, six months in maximum security 23-and-1 lockdown,[2] and six months in minimum-security rehab. There was a chance that I would be turned over to another maximum-security prison until my twenty-first birthday, so I kept my nose clean when I was on the inside and was released on my eighteenth birthday for good behavior.

During the time I was locked up, I tried to make the best of a bad situation. I got my GED and started talking to my dad again. When I was released I had to be in the household of someone who would be responsible for me during my parole, so my dad took on that responsibility. My dad and I started repairing our broken relationship, and I was keeping my nose clean . . . well, for the most part, anyway. I still drank because that didn't show up on my drug tests. Time passed, and I was released from parole. Now that I was no longer under the watchful eye of the authorities, it didn't take long before I started slipping up again. The ground I gained repairing the relationship with my dad was quickly lost, and I was back to living the street life. I never stayed in one place very often because I always quickly wore out my welcome with friends and family.

2. This is where you're locked up for twenty-three hours a day, and free to move around for just one hour.

24

I try to tell myself that if I had only known the short amount of time I had left with my dad, I would have done things differently. But I know it's a lie. I was too self-absorbed for that to be true. I spent my days honestly enough—I somehow managed to maintain a job—but my nights were a different story. They were spent drinking, getting high, and sleeping around with any woman that would have me. I was on an emotional roller coaster destined for hell. I should have seen the signs with my dad: weight loss, pale skin, lack of energy. But like I said, I was too blinded by my own self-centeredness to notice. Shortly after I moved out of my dad's house, he was diagnosed with colon cancer. I watched for the second time as one of my parents was eaten away by cancer and died.

It was right around this time that I found out I was going to be a dad myself. I was head over heels in love with the mother of my child. She could do no wrong in my eyes, even though she was married with two kids and cheating on her husband with me. She was still my beautiful Becca, and I feel so much regret for starting her down a negative path. When she found out she was pregnant, she was dealing with a fresh divorce caused by me and my selfishness, and she didn't want another child. I did, but we both knew I wasn't ready. Still dealing with the blow of my dad's death and the recent turn of events, I tried taking the coward's way out yet again. I swallowed a fistful of Vicodin and chased it with a fifth of liquor, then waited for my own date with death. As you can tell, my date stood me up.

When I finally came around, I found myself strapped to a hospital bed. After a few days of observation and a variety of tests, they cut me loose to return to my insane life. The next few months passed by in a drunken blur, filled with time spent in and out of jail, psych wards, and dark subcultures that society usually overlooks, pretending they don't exist. After my final month in county, I met up with the only sane friend that has stuck by me through thick and thin. Marcus has always been there for me and is more like a brother than anything. He was generous enough to let me stay with him until I could get back on my feet.

A real friend is hard to come by. Marcus has always looked out for me and has always had my best interest at heart. It didn't take long for him to notice that I wasn't going to change my ways, so he had to show me some tough love by telling me to move out. I was tired of living on the street and tired of life in general. I was packing my stuff when I came across a picture of my mom and dad. It seemed like a lifetime had passed since I had them in my life. I broke down and knew I couldn't keep living this way, so I grabbed the nearest knife and started cutting myself, hoping once again to end it all. Marcus stopped me and drove me to the hospital to get the help that I desperately needed.

Looking back at my life of addiction, I was wrong to call the drugs the demon. The true evil presence in my life was me. I wake up every day, look at myself in the mirror, and come to terms with that fact. The insanity and pain that occurred in my life was done by my own hands and through the lusts of my own wicked heart. I thank God for the grace He has extended to me, because only by a loving God's grace could a monster like me have a second chance at life. There is nothing I could ever do to redeem myself from the decisions I have made.

I am by no means perfect now—I still struggle and I still make mistakes—but with God's help I am trying to be a better man. That in and of itself has brought me a long way from the horrible person I used to be. That's all any of us can do: try our best and let God take over the rest.

2

Nobody Dreams of Thirty-Four

Since, then, you have been raised with Christ, set your hearts on things above, where Christ is seated at the right hand of God. Set your minds on things above, not on earthly things. For you died, and your life is now hidden with Christ in God. When Christ, who is your life, appears, then you also will appear with him in glory.

—Colossians 3:1–4

I was twenty years old when I stood at the front of a church and got married. It was the mid-nineties, so I had a little mid-nineties goatee-scruff going that I had carefully cultivated for years. I shaved for the wedding to make my mother-in-law happy, a decision that made me look like a twelve-year-old boy in all my wedding pictures. I had also cut my mid-nineties

Soundgarden[1] hair, which somehow had the effect of making me look like both a twelve-year-old boy and a banker.

At twenty, it's impossible to see beyond a heady mixture of passionate love, sappy declarations of that love, and the kind of raging, drive-hours-in-the-middle-of-the-night-to-see-each-other lust that brings young people together. At twenty, life looks like one long expanse of job offers, wild hotel-room sex, press conferences, and glory, with your Forever 21 hottie wife by your side to see you through it all and pick up your socks.

When you're twenty, you'll occasionally be out on the town with your Forever 21 hottie wife and see an old couple sitting on a park bench. You know what I'm talking about—the feeble but unbelievably content-looking old couple sitting there feeding ducks or playing chess together. You turn to your hottie and say something like, "That's the kind of old couple I want to be. That's going to be us!"[2] At which point she says, "Aww . . ." and then totally wants to make out with you. Life is great when you're twenty.

Fast-forward to thirty-four. Nobody—absolutely nobody—dreams of thirty-four. Thirty-four is what happens between Raging Lust/World is My Oyster and Asexual but Content Feeble Old Couple. Thirty-four is the worst.

It's the worst age because you've lived enough life to see your athletic prowess wane and your body become just a little fatter and a little more unattractive than it was at twenty. You've lived enough life to see that all your dreams aren't

---

1. This was an alt-rock/grunge band in the nineties.
2. You mean this in a completely sincere way when you say it, but you say it in such a way as to suggest, "I want that to be us after we've had sixty years of mind-blowing sex, conquered industry, raised some perfect kids, and lived in Europe. Then we can sit on this park bench and reflect on all the awesome things we've done."

going to come true. You aren't going to play middle linebacker for the Chicago Bears. You aren't going to conquer industry and have a building named after you at your university. Your house isn't that cool. You've never lived in Europe. You still don't have a consistent quiet time. Your kids make you mad. The house is always dirty. The lawn needs to be mowed.

At twenty, change is a fact of life. You live life in semester-long chunks. No cute girls in your classes this semester? No problem! You'll get a new set of classes and girls in a few months! Hate your professor? No problem! Change your major! Change goes hand-in-hand with being young, and change is exciting.

At thirty-four, however, change is a tremendously hard thing to pull off. For one thing, you said the words "till death do us part" in front of God and a roomful of witnesses. That feels different at thirty-four than it did at twenty. There's a sense of, well, *finality* to it. A finality that, admittedly, comes with a lot of great perks—a person who knows you intuitively because you've spent thirteen great years together. A person who loves you and who is loyal to you. I adore my wife and thank God for her, but sometimes I think she got the short end of the stick when she married me.

At thirty-four you can't just quit your job, break your apartment lease, and move someplace else just because you like the idea of moving someplace else. You can't do the obligatory young, evangelical post-college year in Chicago (or Europe[3]) that you should have done before you had these commitments. You can't do a lot of things.

3. We actually DID do this. We lived in Lithuania for a year right after college, where we taught in a school for missionary kids. Though rather than "get adventure out of our system," I think it just whetted our appetite for it and maybe made everything else seem boring by comparison.

Dallas and the Spitfire

By thirty-four, some of the big, important things you wanted to do haven't worked out. Sometimes this is minor, like not having the luxury of touring Europe. Other times it's life-changing and tragic. My own recent major loss was when we were trying to adopt my son Maxim's biological sister. We did paperwork, paid thousands, prayed, and hoped for this little girl to be reunited with her biological brother, only to be told that because of a loophole in some Ukrainian legislation, a Ukrainian family moved to adopt her (despite our pleadings to the contrary). The whole thing was heartbreaking and shook our faith probably more than any one life circumstance has ever shaken our faith. What was especially hard was the idea that God would show us something that was a blessing (a daughter), we would thank Him for it, and then He would—seemingly without good reason—take it away from us. Our initial reaction was to get really cynical about this event, and about God. But the more I think about it, the more I think our only two real options are to curse God and die, or to continue to faithfully try to love and serve Him, even in the midst of the heartbreak, and even though it seemingly happened for no good reason. We continue to pray that He shows us His plan for all of it, and that He redeems it.

At thirty-four—and maybe at any age—the spiritual landscape is tough. Something I've been mulling over lately is the idea that as evangelical men, we (not just you and I, but the royal, evangelical WE) equate being spiritually "good" with not looking at porn. Porn has become the enemy, to the degree that, in our minds, a "good" week spiritually means I didn't look at porn and a bad week means I did. But there are a lot of other sins and spiritual issues that need tending to as well: our prayer lives, our ability to trust in God, our tempers, our attitudes, etc. And something else I'm mulling over is the fact that I may very well indeed be "brokenhearted" as in the kind of brokenheartedness described in Psalm 13.[4] That is, I'm not down for any particular definable reason, just semi-heartbroken . . . feeling sometimes like the Lord has forgotten me.

One reminder that He hasn't completely forgotten me is a quasi-discipleship relationship I have with a pastor friend of mine named Cory. Cory and I went to college together. He was the kid with the dorm room so clean that you could eat off the floor. There were never clothes strewn about the room, and whenever I would come into his room to talk, he and his roommate, Brent, would be at their desks studying quietly. This was almost creepy. Cory and I started talking as freshmen and have never really stopped. We talk weekly for at least an hour, and pray for one another. He's a pastor now, and he seemed to be a good person to go to when I wanted/ needed to start thinking about discipleship.

"One thing I'm wrestling with is the relationship between discipleship and catechesis (defined here as 'transferring doctrine to a new mind,' not as memorization of a

---

4. How long, LORD? Will you forget me forever?
   How long will you hide your face from me?
   How long must I wrestle with my thoughts
   and every day have sorrow in my heart?
   How long will my enemy triumph over me?

   Look on me and answer, O LORD my God.
   Give light to my eyes, or I will sleep in death;
   my enemy will say, "I have overcome him,"
   and my foes will rejoice when I fall.

   But I trust in your unfailing love;
   my heart rejoices in your salvation.
   I will sing to the LORD,
   for he has been good to me.

question-and-answer catechism per se)," Cory writes. *"It seems the silent assumption everywhere, including often in my own head, is that they are the same thing. How do you disciple someone? Throw him in a class? Give him a book?"*[5]

It becomes clear early on that Dallas's needs transcend being thrown in a class, given a book to read, or even a once-a-week coffee and accountability deal. What Dallas really needs is a friend. And maybe even more, what he really, really needs is a father. Thankfully our hope and trust is in our heavenly Father, who can provide more abundantly for Dallas than I could ever hope or imagine.

The book-and-coffee model of discipleship seems semi-absurd to me, partly because we don't see Jesus doing this. Jesus taught, He led by example, He came alongside, and He healed. Of course, He also had the distinct advantage of being sinless, all-knowing, and the Son of God. I am none of these. It's clear to me that I'll have to learn to disciple Dallas by mimicking the person who discipled me: my dad. He was far from perfect—and in fact I would argue that his honesty about his imperfections made him an even better discipler—but the way he talked with me, listened to me, and spent time with me will provide a road map for my time with Dallas.

"I was a disciple of my piano teachers," Cory writes. *"Interestingly, though I benefited enormously (and necessarily) from my first and third teachers who drilled me on technique, I think I matured the most in the shortest period of time with my second teacher. Most of our lessons were spent talking,*

5. Books I've given Dallas: *Spiritual Depression* by D. Martyn Lloyd-Jones; *The Mortification of Sin* by John Owen; *Hello, I Love You: Adventures in Adoptive Fatherhood* by Ted Kluck; *Facing Tyson: Fifteen Fighters, Fifteen Stories* by Ted Kluck; and *Hero of the Underground* by a former heroin/coke/painkiller addict named Christian Peter.

*and when it came to the playing, he played more than I did.
But I became more and more like him as a pianist because I
spent time with him and picked up his way of doing things.
That's discipleship. Incidentally, it occurred to me that while
Dallas is your disciple in the Way of Jesus, you are his disciple
in the Way of Auto Repair."*

I wonder where my relationship with Dallas fits into the
life of the church, whether I'm talking about Sunday morning corporate worship or the smaller context of our Tuesday
night Growth Group. That is, where does a relationship that
seems so personal (discipleship) fit into the larger context of
church life?

*"What I'm really trying to grasp is what these and other
jumbled questions mean for discipleship in the church,"* Pastor Cory writes. *"Discipleship as I've begun to define it here is
intrinsically relational. Because we're finite beings, the number of people we can disciple is small. Because we're diverse
beings living diverse lives, the degree to which we can design
a step-by-step guide to discipleship is limited."*

So as ridiculous as it would be to write a book about discipleship that is built around weekly meetings at Starbucks, it
would be equally ridiculous to suggest that all guys should buy
old cars and fix them up together as a means of discipleship.
The fact of the matter is that both Dallas and I are interested
in cars, and the car has become our reason for talking and
getting together. The discussions about life, women, theology,
and the future will all happen around the car.

*"All of this points to the main outcome of discipleship
being the development of a person who is trustworthy and
wise enough to disciple someone else,"* Cory writes. *"Jesus's instruction of the Twelve as we see it in the Gospels*

is small-scale, relational, spontaneous, reactive, hands-on, nonliterate, and largely nonlinear in content delivery.

"Then there's the role of the Holy Spirit in discipleship. At times, Paul and his companions would plant a church, appoint elders, and take off in what we would consider a shockingly short time for someone to go from pagan to Christian leader/ teacher. But they seemed to be confident that what they didn't have time to do in person was well within the capacity of the Holy Spirit, whose job was to 'guide [disciples] into all truth' (John 16:13–15, cf. 1 John 2:20–27). Do our attempts at discipleship demonstrate any trust that the Holy Spirit teaches people? Or are we content making catechumens that display no evidence of the Holy Spirit in their lives?"

Thankfully, I've seen Dallas benefitting from both types—catechesis and discipleship. Or to put it another way, head knowledge and heart transformation. And it would be downright foolish to deny the work of the Holy Spirit in his life. His changes have been so drastic that it HAS to be the Holy Spirit at work. I've seen him absorbing teaching from the pulpit and from church programs like a sponge, but I've also seen the tangible benefit of his one-to-one relationship with me. And I see the same things in myself. I need great, meaty, solid, biblically-saturated preaching, but I also need to be able to talk to people once in a while. But, ironically, it may be the over-programming that's contributing to the state of semi-burnout that I'm finding myself in.

Church life is a sea of commitments. For example, Kristin and I lead a Bible study in our home every other Tuesday, cook a dinner for fifty Chinese people at church every Wednesday, teach the college Sunday school class on Sunday morning, and this month are working the toddler room, which means that we referee the *Lord of the Flies* scenario that happens when thirty-two kids[6] between the ages of two to four gather in a small room in our church that is filled with toys and other toddler stuff. Chaos ensues. I would rather be beaten with sticks than work in the toddler room.

I run down that litany of responsibilities not in an "I'm so busy" way, but in a way that illustrates that when you're thirty-four you're doing a lot of work for a lot of people. There are a lot of people to keep happy.

Michael Duffy, age seventeen, is a homeschooled kid from my church and has a knowledge of cars that borders on encyclopedic. His dad is an engineer from GM, so Michael has been reading car catalogs and magazines since the cradle. He's also super-passionate about this stuff and thinks my project is cool, so naturally I've invited him to go and look at a car with me. Dallas is away at Bible college, so he pitches in on the car search via email and Facebook, but I felt like I needed Michael's expert eye so that I didn't overlook something obvious.[7]

Michael defies several stereotypes, but the main one is the fact that homeschooled kids are somehow less socially adjusted than their otherwise-schooled counterparts. In short, he's cooler than 99 percent of the guys I usually hang out with, and he's up for an adventure.

Part of what's cool about searching for a vintage European convertible, as opposed to, say, a Ford Mustang, is that they're few and far between, so there is some real searching

---

6. That represents, like, four families at our church.
7. Like a hole in the floorboards. I actually overlooked this on a car once.

involved. At church, Michael shared with me that he had a lead on a 1980 Triumph TR-7, owned by some vintage toy dealer in his neighborhood. This guy, apparently, is a trader in old toys and has been trying to get rid of his Triumph for a couple of years. This could be good.

The Triumph Motor Company is a British manufacturer, also known at various times for motorcycles and bicycles. The TR-7 was characterized by its wedge shape and looks not-unlike a Pontiac Fiero. However, stateside demand was so high for the TR-7 that in 1974 it actually delayed the car's release in Great Britain. All told, there were over 112,000 of these produced, which doesn't sound like that many, really. I kind of dig the idea of having something that not many people have.

"It might be too nice for you, though," Michael says, cognizant of the fact that I'm looking for something that needs to be fixed up a little, but not something that is an overwhelming disaster. This is a fine line.

The car sits out in front of a mostly empty strip mall. This is something that Michigan has a lot of lately (the mostly empty strip malls), due to our anemic economy. The car is even tinier looking in real life than it is in photographs . . . this being the first time I've laid eyes, or hands, on an actual Triumph.

It's bright orange and, like most '80s sports cars, it has some kind of a dumb graphic (a garish racing stripe, or the name of the car model, or both) on the side. The body appears to be in great shape, and because of friends like Michael, I've learned how to crawl underneath a vehicle to look inside the wheel wells, underneath floor pans, and underneath the carpet inside a car to see what kind of shape the body is in. This car, as we feared, appears to be nearly perfect. On a whim, I try the door handle—it's unlocked. People in Dewitt, Michigan, are apparently very trusting.

It's the inside of the vehicle that's most disappointing. The upholstery and dash are very unremarkable, meaning that they don't look at all European or cool. It looks like the inside of a Fiero or a Nissan or any other run-of-the-mill car that it has an all-plastic dash and wheel, boring gauges, and taupe[8] fabric on the seats. These are easily remedied, but unfortunately the engine is in perfect shape.

"I don't think people want to read a book about buying new carpet for the inside of a car," Michael explains. "This needs to look like the kind of European convertible a fashion model or James Bond might step out of," he says.

This makes me wonder what homeschooled-Michael knows about European fashion models. However, I totally agree that the car needs to have a certain stylish, impractical vibe. Translation: It needs to have a wood dashboard, cool-looking gauges, and leather seats. It needs to be the type of car you'd wear gloves while driving, for absolutely no reason at all besides fashion. These, I'm learning, are nonnegotiables. It's good to get this figured out.

Our next stop is a vintage car place on the north side of Lansing, in a weird neighborhood by the airport. This is an airport that tries to bill itself as "International" (read: flights to Toronto), but it is really just three gates and a diner. The neighborhood is a strange amalgam of modern fast-food options, used-car joints, and old greasy-spoon eateries.

---

8. I have an especially strained relationship with the color beige. I hate it. It feels like it wants to be a color but isn't, or that it wants to be white but isn't. Beige is safe and boring.

Dallas and the Spitfire

Michael: "I don't think I'd ever eat food that came out of a place called 'Mijo's' and looked like that." "That" being dirty and condemned-looking, as though Mijo was produc-ing the food in his own kitchen, replete with an old radio, empty beer bottles lying around, and dirty dishes that had been there for an undisclosed amount of time.

The vintage car place looks completely deserted except for a neon Open sign. Inside the showroom is an assortment of Fiats and Triumph convertibles. This bodes well. There is an old guy sitting motionless in a chair inside the showroom. We walk up to the front door, on which there is a sign that reads "Out of Order." The door? The whole place? The guy points us to a side door near the garage through which we will pass and then enter a different decade. No chirping telephones. No mechanical sounds. No Muzak. No computer terminals. It's completely silent.

The guy becomes friendly and animated when we show interest in his cars. He is like a mechanic in a Norman Rock-well painting. Tall. Angular. There's something Marlboro-manish about him as well. I imagine him showing his own grandkids around this place, and the grandkids climbing all over the cars in a way that makes him swell with pride but also feel nervous.

I feel, for a moment, like I am back in my grandfather's garage in Plainfield, Illinois. There are calendars hanging on the walls from the 1980s, yellowing with age. There are ash-trays because old guys still smoke. There are parts catalogs for old cars that nobody is buying (besides us) and nobody is driving. These guys are committed to the past. Super com-mitted. It's as though they've decided that the present is too difficult and complicated, and as a result they have resolved to hanging out here, in this garage, which represents (and actually IS) the past. I feel a little judgmental, and then I feel jealous. Weird.

Michael and I both notice the creepy motionless guy sitting on a sofa in the back of the dark room. He could be a prop in a diorama on the Great Depression. In fact, I think—irrationally—that he is a mannequin, until he actually moves a little bit. He never speaks to us. Michael raises his eyebrows. This is a lot of adventure for a homeschooled kid with an outsized love of cars.

The other guy (Rockwell) shows us his collection of Fiats and Triumphs. It's awesome. He tells us of driving with the top down in the summer, and I imagine him doing so, hoping that he has a woman to share the experience with. These European cars were made for love . . . which is one reason why I'm so attracted to them.

3

Not Afraid

Therefore, as God's chosen people, holy and dearly loved, clothe yourselves with compassion, kindness, humility, gentleness and patience. Bear with each other and forgive whatever grievances you may have against one another. Forgive as the Lord forgave you. And over all these virtues put on love, which binds them all together in perfect unity.

—Colossians 3:12–14

● MY SALVATION STORY—BY DALLAS ●

I knew I was at the bottom of the barrel. I was on my third suicide attempt, lying in the hospital, feeling like my body was being ripped apart from the inside out as I was withdrawing from all the different drugs and alcohol in my body. There was nothing to ease the pain except the assurance that the pain and cold sweats would ease as the days went by. I slipped in and out of consciousness the first couple of days, then the worst seemed to be over. I was in the psych ward for observation when they broke the news to me. The doctors and my probation officer refused to release me from the hospital until I found a long-term in-patient rehab to get some serious help. Thoughts raced through my mind, thoughts of trying to fight my way out, thoughts of trying to end it all again. Finally, I snapped. "What do you mean you're not going to release me? I'm leaving one way or the other!" Now, when you look the way I did, that kind of statement doesn't go over too well with security. The next thing I knew, I was being held down and getting a shot pumped into my backside to knock me out.

When I finally came around after my drug-induced nap, I was a lot calmer and started thinking things through. I needed to get out of there, but it was definitely not going to be on my terms, so I decided to play their little game. I jumped through the hoops and went to the meetings they wanted me to, and waited as my caseworker made call after call and was rejected time after time because of my violent history and unstable character. It seemed like I was never going to get out of there. I wasn't a very social person. Actually, to be honest, I was a self-centered, arrogant jerk—at least that's what all my ex-girlfriends told me—but I got bored so I started talking with the other patients in the common area. That's when I met Villam, a tall, skinny, white South African guy with a thick accent. As weird as he seemed to me, I thought he was pretty cool, so we talked for quite a while trading stories about life and trying to pass the time. That's when he shared the Gospel with me. I thought, This guy really is crazy! He's sitting next to me in the psych ward, telling me that if I believe in some dead guy, I could live forever. I lost my temper and told him to mind his own business, and went back to my room.

I will never forget the chain of events that unfolded after that conversation with Villam. I had been lying in my room for about an hour or so when I heard a faint knock on my door. Before I could answer, in walked some black guy wearing a cheap suit and fedora. As I sat up, he told me in a thick Caribbean accent that he was a chaplain from the hospital, and he wanted to talk to me about a few things. I thought, Here we go again, as he dove into his story about his childhood in the Caribbean islands. He told me about growing up in poverty and wanting to have a better life, and then he switched the focus to his older brother, who received a very generous offer from a wealthy neighbor to pay for an education and a new life in America. He told me that his brother refused because of the thug lifestyle he led. The Caribbean guy used this story as a comparison to my situation as he told me that Jesus could give me new life if I would only take advantage of His gift to me. He asked if I had an opportunity like that, would I take advantage of it or let it slip by? I was thinking, What is up with all these foreign psychos wanting me to worship somebody who has been dead for two thousand years? But being the well-mannered gentleman that I was, I told him to get out of my room and save his religion for somebody who cared.

This is when God really intervened and pulled me to himself in a huge way. As I told you before, my caseworker had been calling around for days trying to get me into rehab with no luck at all. About twenty minutes after I'd kicked the Caribbean guy out of my room, in walked my caseworker smiling ear to ear. She told me she had an amazing opportunity for me but I needed to stay open-minded. I asked her what she was talking about, and she told me that she found a place that would take me in! When I asked her why I needed to stay open-minded, she explained that it was a yearlong in-patient Bible-based rehab. All I could think was, You have to be kidding me! But my interest in getting out of the psych ward overrode my disinterest in God, so I got on the phone and talked to Rich Gray, the program director of the Lansing City Rescue Mission, and told him I was interested.

Dallas and the Spitfire

Now I had a new obstacle in my path: How was I going to get a supervised ride from Ann Arbor to Lansing? I knew it was a long shot, but I called my probation officer and told him I found a place that would take me in, but I needed a ride to Lansing. He put me on hold to talk to my judge, and somehow he got it approved. On July 1, via police and a probation officer escort, my journey began to what I thought was going to be Bible boot camp for burnouts.

When we got to the Mission, what I saw was definitely not the image I had in my mind. The building is wedged between a variety of stores in downtown Lansing; the only thing that sets it apart is the cross on the front with red letters saying "Jesus saves." All I kept thinking as I walked in was, What did I get myself into? After getting my intake paperwork done, Rich showed me to my bunk upstairs, where I immediately crashed. I spent the following days trying to adjust to my new surroundings. The guys in there with me were all seasoned vets when it came to living the street life, but I noticed something different about some of them when we swapped stories. They kept bringing up God and how things are so different for them now that He was in their lives. I went through the motions for the first couple of days, going to devotions and classes without really paying attention.

On July 5, the day after celebrating our country's independence, I realized just how dependent I needed to become. In the pastor's office, after hearing a message full of hope, forgiveness, and love, I turned my life over to Jesus Christ as my Lord and Savior. After seeing firsthand the impact Christ had on the guys I was now bunking with and hearing this offer of a new life, I could no longer resist the amazing grace that God had extended to me. I will never forget that night; it was filled with tears of joy and tears of regret over the fact that I had resisted so long. I knew things would be different from then on—I didn't know how, but I knew they would. I never could have guessed how different, though, as I spent the next year going through an incredible transformation spiritually and physically. The year I spent in the program in the mission was by far the best year of my life up to that point. I spent my twenty-first birthday not at the bar but at a baptism. The newfound joy I had now in life was incredible.

I've put my search on hiatus long enough to get Dallas ready to go to Bible school. The school connection was brokered by the director of the Lansing City Rescue Mission, and while we're all excited for his opportunity, the school freaks us out a little bit. We spend one tense evening around the dinner table, leafing through a rule booklet that came with his enrollment papers.

The positives: The school is, literally, in the middle of nowhere[1] in Northern Michigan, which (the middle of nowhere) can be really charming, and can also be good for someone who is trying to stay free and clear of the drug culture that pervades many urban areas. Also, Dallas will get to study Scripture for the majority of his days, cultivating his gifts for preaching and ministry.

The negatives: It's really conservative. And by conservative I mean that Dallas isn't allowed to wear T-shirts with anything printed on them, isn't allowed to bring any popular music (secular or Christian) to campus, has to wear khakis and a golf shirt[2] to classes, has to wear a suit to church, can

1. It's in Prudenville, which, somewhat appropriately, has the word *prude* in it . . . appropriate given the next paragraph.
2. I hate khakis and a golf shirt. This is the fashion equivalent to the color beige and is, I feel, the required uniform for people who have no taste or creativity. (See above.)

only read the King Jimmy,[3] and will basically be trapped on campus with thirty to forty other fundamentalists for an entire school year. Just thinking about all of these rules is enough to make my head explode.

"They're going to love Dallas up there," explains Zach, my American Baptist pastor friend. "There's nothing a conservative Baptist loves more than a testimony like Dallas's. Those testimonies are like crack cocaine to a fundie."

An interesting metaphor, given Dallas's past. The reality is that he's having serious second thoughts about going up to school, as well as second thoughts about whether ministry is his calling to begin with.

"I love working for Johnny," Dallas says. Johnny is our friend Jon, who runs his own construction company and for whom Dallas has enjoyed working all summer. Dallas, in addition to being a talented mechanic, is great at construction. He loves working hard and has enjoyed living a normal-ish life this summer—working for Jon, coming to our small group, and going to church on Sundays.

"I could see doing this . . . doing construction . . . for the rest of my life," he says. We are standing outside in front of my house by a truck that he purchased for a few hundred of the bucks he earned working for Jon. The truck is a piece of junk, but Dallas is the kind of guy who can buy a piece of junk for a few hundred dollars and keep it running. He

3. The King James Version of the Bible. If you're a Reformed person, like I am, the ESV Study Bible (Crossway) is the only modern Bible translation you acknowledge. You may not be able to articulate why, exactly, you like it or how, exactly, it differs from the NIV (which, by the way, was the only Bible to use fifteen years ago . . . total disclosure: I still read an NIV on most days) or the NASB (which was the only Bible to use five years ago). But that doesn't matter. All you know is that you're supposed to use the ESV and rave about it, so you do. Until the next version comes out.

has purchased a pack of cigarettes and is smoking one by the truck. He does this when he's stressed. We've decided, together, not to fight this battle (tobacco). Sobriety-wise, we feel he's still on the right track. Although if he goes to school, the cigarettes will stay here.

"I feel like I'm the Great White Hope," he says, referring to his reputation at the rescue mission. "The failure rate is huge at places like that. Most guys who go through the program and get clean end up relapsing. They really want me to go into ministry; they really like telling my story because I think it helps them raise money."

On the one hand, I'm proud of my friend's savvy. For such a young guy, he has an incredible grasp of the real issues at hand. However, I also feel, deep down, that the Mission isn't trying to use him. I think they're just encouraged by finally having something/someone to be encouraged about. And I think they see a ton of potential—both for spiritual growth and a ministry career—in my friend. These are heavy issues.

"Try not to think of it as a spiritual issue," I tell Dallas. "What I mean is that if you decide to stay here and work construction, you're not doing anything 'unspiritual.' You can honor God with your life if you go to work for Johnny every day, work hard, and enjoy your involvement in the church. You could also honor God if you decide to go to LiveRight. I don't think it's an either/or type of thing."

Our small group—we've all taken on a sort of parental role with Dallas—is split as to whether the Bible school is a good option for him. My wife thinks he's going to go up there and find a little Baptist hottie with whom to settle down.

"Dallas has never been able to hang around with Christians his own age," she says. "Besides, it's going to be fish in a barrel for him up there with his tattoos and 'mysterious past' and stuff. He'll be fending them[4] off with a stick."

I hear what she's saying. Dallas exists in a strange netherworld in our church. He hangs out with us and some of the other young couples, but for the most part, people his age are either getting their PhDs or they've left the area for jobs elsewhere. He tried the Spartan Christian Fellowship college group, but it didn't take. The differences between "recovering drug addict" and "affluent young John Piper fan" were just a little too much to overcome. At least for the moment.

———

Dallas has decided to go to the Bible college just days before he is required to be there. As such, he needs a new wardrobe, and fast. My friend Dan and I have taken it upon ourselves to take Dallas shopping and outfit him. It's like *What Not to Wear* for Midwestern guys. Dan, the director of computer security for the entire state of Michigan, is one of the most enthusiastic people on the planet. He's also a loud talker. Before long, everyone in JCPenney knows who we are and what we're doing. We've drawn an audience. We're giving fashion advice to old ladies and picking out ties for wives to give to their husbands. It takes a village . . . I'm having more fun than I've had in a long time. This is a blast.

We've outfitted Dallas in a sharp-looking suit, including dress socks, dress shoes, a dress belt, and lots of dress shirts with which to cover up his tats. We've spent way too much time debating cotton vs. broadcloth, weighing their relative merits. I've had a completely un-ironic conversation with Dan about the merits of dress shirts that have colored or

4. Baptist hotties.

patterned bodies but white collars. We sound like a couple of chicks.

We're on our way out of Penneys when I pass a display of golf shirts that don't look like they belong on a schlumpy middle manager somewhere. I point the black one out to Dallas.

"That shirt is sick," he says. I grab it and add it to our haul. Everybody should have at least one golf shirt that looks sick and that they're not embarrassed to wear.

My friend Ben and I are driving Dallas up to school—Ben riding with Dallas, and me following behind in my own car. Ben is a stay-at-home dad and, as such, is the only other guy in the small group with the flexibility to do this on a weekday. The previous night, our small group sent Dallas off in style, with all of the sheets, laundry baskets, shampoo, and snacks he could possibly need for a year at school. My eight-year-old son, Tristan, even got into the act, using his allowance money to buy Dallas a bag of Cheetos.

I have mixed feelings. I'm sad to see my friend go, but excited for his opportunity to hole up with Scripture for a year. I'm also a little worried about what the school will look and feel like. I'm expecting sad-looking women in burlap dresses and classroom buildings that look like pole barns. One thing I'm not worried about, though, is Dallas's academic performance.

"I've been reading at a college level ever since fifth grade," he explains. "In fifth grade I had the second-highest MEAP[5] score in the school, next to some Asian kid. And with the art scholarships I had and the academic money that would

5. Michigan Educational Assessment Program.

have been available, I pretty much could have gone anywhere to school. I was stupid."

Our trip is uneventful, except for a moment in which Dallas and Ben pull Dallas's truck over to the shoulder of the highway. I'm crestfallen. Ben and I have zero mechanical skills between us. There are grade-school girls who know their way around vehicles better than we do. This is not good.

"What happened?" I ask as Dallas exits his vehicle. I'm imagining cops driving by and pulling over, running his license through their computers and then searching the vehicle. "Is your truck okay?"

"Yeah, it's fine," he says. "I tried to throw my cigarette out the window and it flew back in."

I roll my eyes and we resume the trip.

In a word, the campus is amazing. It's less a campus and more a collection of sharp-looking log cabins in the middle of the woods near Houghton Lake. There's a cafeteria, a coffee shop, and a gymnasium. I'm immediately transported back to summer camp. The buildings look nice, and the people seem normal. This could be good.

"I think Benny and I need to stay here and chill out for a few days," I explain to Dallas. This would be a great place to hang out and read a book or ten. We head into the office to get him officially registered and settled.

"And how do you know Dallas?" asks the nice lady behind the desk.

"We're his parents," I deadpan. Benny plays along, smiling. For a moment the secretaries are crestfallen, and then we smile and they all laugh, relieved. I'm buoyed by the fact that everyone we've met seems normal and nice. It's not what I'd expected at all.

We walk through the dormitories (cabins), and I can tell that Dallas is nervous. This is all exceedingly new to him. We walk past a gigantic pile of wood. "Say hello to your work study job," says Benny.

We leave with little pomp and circumstance, which is pretty much the way it usually works when guys are taking care of other guys. It's raining and we give Dallas a hug in front of his dormitory before starting the long ride back to Lansing.

―――――

A white, tough-looking little 1977 MGB is sitting outside a brick building in Eaton Rapids, Michigan. The brick building, which looks like it was built in the '40s or '50s, is adjacent to a neon and brick Rite Aid drugstore, which looks like it was built last week.

MGBs are small British four-cylinder sports cars that were designed to compete with Triumph's TR series. And when I say small, I mean it. This thing is tiny; not only is the cockpit cramped (see: elbows and knees touching when hands are on steering wheel), the engine compartment is even more cramped, meaning that I can't imagine my average-sized hands inside it to work on anything. Almost half a million of these babies were produced, and over a third of them are still on the road today. You can get a pristine, restored MGB for around twenty grand, but there are a ton of them available, like this one, for under five thousand dollars.

It occurs to me that using Craigslist to look for cars is a weird way to meet the General Public.[6] In the interest of total disclosure, I'm usually not real excited about meeting the General Public—I became a self-employed writer for a

6. This is a catch-all term I often use to describe people I don't know.

reason. I expect GP folks who are selling cars to be flinty-eyed, grizzled, and way more experienced with this stuff than I am.

Jamey, the guy selling the car, is the exact opposite. He's about my age, is dressed like me, and is simply trying to unload a collection of old cars that belonged to his deceased father-in-law. He opens a door to the old building, which, as it turns out, was something of a warehouse for his father-in-law's hobbies and hoardings.

"This used to be a used-book store," he explains, gesturing at a treasure trove of used books. There are few things I love more than browsing used-book stores, and my eyes light up like saucers. I'm suddenly way less interested in looking at cars.

"I could spend hours in here," I reply. I'm already warming to the idea of buying the car from this guy, due to the serious literary vibes in the place. When you know nothing about cars, these are the feelings you rely on. Thankfully I have Gary, a friend and auto nut, with me to assess the condition of the car. Gary is a corrections officer and looks like Wyatt Earp, mustache-wise. He's the last person on earth anyone would rip off, for fear of serious retribution. Also, we drove to the appointment in his pristine '71 Buick. It's impossible not to gain fifteen pounds of lean muscle mass just by riding in a car like that.[7]

Jamey leads us down a dark hallway that opens into a back garage that contains an old Austin-Healey, two broken down "parts" MGBs, and a couple of pristine-looking late-model Mercedes coupes. Finally, we go outside and get a glimpse

---

7. We'll find a back road later on which to do burnouts—both of us hollering and giggling like teenagers listening to the squeal of tires on pavement and the throaty rumble of the engine.

of the white MGB. There's a reason why the Internet photos looked so good—all of the quarter panels had been replaced, which accounts for the lack of surface rust. The inside—engine compartments and floor panels—is another story.

"This is at least a three-year project," says Gary, crawling around the car like he was born crawling around cars. "Under the hood it's a little bit of a mess." I do what I do, which is look into the engine compartment dumbly and nod at what I feel are the appropriate times. I'm getting that anxious feeling that I get whenever I'm about to get myself in way over my head. It's the same feeling I felt on my first day as a professional indoor football player.

"This is what I do, Gary," I tell him. "I get in over my head, and then I dig my way out." I say this with a mixture of pride, shame, and fear.

4

Patiently Waiting
for a Book to Explode On

*Jimmy was the kind of guy that rooted for bad guys
in the movies.*

—Henry Hill, *Goodfellas*

*Put to death, therefore, whatever belongs to your earthly
nature: sexual immorality, impurity, lust, evil desires
and greed, which is idolatry. Because of these, the wrath
of God is coming. You used to walk in these ways, in the
life you once lived. But now you must rid yourselves of
all such things as these: anger, rage, malice, slander, and
filthy language from your lips. Do not lie to each other,
since you have taken off your old self with its practices
and have put on the new self, which is being renewed
in knowledge in the image of its Creator.*

—Colossians 3:5–11

Dallas, home for the weekend from Bible school, is standing in my kitchen where my wife is making dinner, and

we're talking about cocaine. I ask him how old he was when he first used.

"I was young . . . eleven or twelve, I suppose," he says. I ask him how it made him feel. It occurs to me that I've interviewed a ton of drug addicts in my years as a sportswriter, but I'd never asked how it made them feel.

"It made me feel like a locomotive was running through my brain," he says. "It was pretty much instant euphoria. You get a ton of energy, and you become ultra-aware of your surroundings. The problem wasn't the drug, though," he adds. "The problem was me. I had pretty much quit life by that point. . . . I just wanted to shut it down every night."

Kristin and I ponder this for a moment. She is rolling out dough for Crescent Rolls. It strikes me that our life must seem astonishingly boring to Dallas. I wonder aloud—because it's the only thing I can think to wonder—how he could afford a coke habit as a poor white teenager. Not aloud—inside— I'm wondering how Jesus can measure up to the feeling of freight-train euphoria that comes from cocaine.[1] One of the reasons it's dangerous is that, like any idol, it becomes a person's replacement for God.

According to Wikipedia, "Cocaine is a powerful nervous system stimulant. Its effects can last from 15–30 minutes to an hour, depending upon the method of ingestion. Cocaine increases alertness, feelings of well-being and euphoria, energy and motor activity, feelings of competence and sexuality. Athletic performance may be enhanced in sports where sustained attention and endurance is required. Anxiety, paranoia and restlessness are also frequent. With excessive dosage,

1. Alone in my office, thinking about this later, I am brought to tears. I'm also listening to R.E.M.'s "Night Swimming," which may have something to do with it.

tremors, convulsions and increased body temperature are observed."[2]

The problem is that it makes its users feel like a million bucks, which of course leads to debilitating dependency and addiction. So how does a kid from the streets with no money or connections acquire it?

"It depends who you know," he says of the cost. "That's why I started running with the people I did—for the connections."

At the peak of his cocaine consumption, Dallas was living in a small town in Ohio, where he became a middleman for the area's most prominent coke dealer. "I was working at a Bob Evans as a dishwasher," he explains. "And I sold coke to literally everybody on my shift. Everybody at Bob Evans was high. I would hide little dime bags of coke in the little lip thing on the inside of my cap. Everybody would take their breaks at different times, and then go into the bathroom and do lines off the back of the toilet.

"The parties were outrageous," he says. "Like a scene out of *Scarface*. There would literally be a huge pile of blow on a coffee table and we'd all be sitting around snorting and watching music videos. The girls liked to freebase . . . and sometimes they would just dip the ends of their cigarettes into the coke. I was with so many girls. . . . I'm surprised I never got anything.[3] But I've been good about getting tested."

This is such a mind-blowing departure from the kinds of drug use I've been exposed to before. At my upscale Christian college in Indiana, the drug use generally involved rich suburban kids covertly driving into Muncie to buy one-hit bongs at used-record stores and then covertly planning their

2. http://en.wikipedia.org/wiki/Cocaine
3. Talking sexually transmitted diseases here.

"getting high" scenarios in such a way that it (the scenario[4]) was almost as exciting and buzz-inducing as the getting-high itself. And as an athlete, I'm used to the upper/downer cycle that some guys indulged in—using a variety of "drines" to psych-up, or a variety of low-grade "downers" to come down after games, which, believe it or not, is exceedingly hard after your body has been jacked on adrenaline for three-plus hours. But this, Dallas's drug use, is a whole 'nother (so to speak) ballgame.

Kristin asks Dallas about prison.

"The longest I was in was thirteen months straight," he says. "That was maximum security, which meant that we were locked in our rooms for twenty-three hours, with one hour of rec time. They let us have books in there once in a while, but I mostly just had a lot of time to think and talk. My roommate was a big Mexican guy named Ortiz.

"I had an agreement with the guards," he continues. "They would bring us cigarettes and dip[5] as long as I kept the guys calm. So occasionally I would have to take a guy into the bathroom and straighten him out to keep the benefits coming. But the guards trusted me, and they gave me extra privileges, like after everybody went to sleep I could stay up and watch TV."

Dallas was bigger and tougher than everybody else, so it makes sense that he was the de facto enforcer inside, but he's also been blessed with the gift of gab. He's a good talker, and I'm not at all surprised that the prison guards trusted him.

"I think prison guard is a way tougher job than cop," he says. "Prison guards are around dangerous people all day,

---

4. All of that to say, for them it was more about the subculture than addiction, where life becomes all about acquiring the drug.

5. Chewing tobacco. That really gross stuff that kids in your high school would chew and then spit into empty pop bottles.

every day. And I know that some of them wanted to show us compassion and maybe even share the gospel . . . but if you show even the slightest bit of vulnerability, the inmates will take advantage of it and eat you alive. I've seen it happen with the younger guards. You almost have to get completely jaded and cynical before you can do that job well."

As Dallas is telling me this, I'm flipping through pictures he brought—pictures of Dallas with his brother and his friend Marcus when he first got to the mission. He looks different. His shaven head was just starting to grow out, and his brother, looking like a slightly older version of Dallas, was beside him holding a baby. There is a fifth-grade school picture of Dallas—the kind of picture they take of every kid during the fall when a photographer comes into school and gives everybody a black plastic comb. There's nothing about the school picture that says "future coke dealer."

The photo album still has his inmate number written on the cover in black Sharpie. "I cried like a baby when I got that photo album in prison," he says. "I missed my niece so much.

"Inside, everybody was involved with gang activity at some level," he says. "In order for people to leave you alone, you had to walk this fine line between not being too quiet—because if you were too quiet they'd eat you alive—and not being too tough-guy cocky, because then everybody wants to try[6] you. I got jumped in my cell by these guys who wanted me to join their gang. I refused because I was already involved with some other people, and I ended up having to find them all, one by one, and take care of it.[7] Then nobody ever messed with me again."

6. Read: fight.
7. Read: fight them.

He even speaks of inmates taking fruit from the commissary and letting it ferment in the toilets in their cells, making a kind of home-brewed hooch. I'm silent. Finally I wonder if, inside, he ever had a desire to get clean and turn his life around.

"I thought about it," he says, "but when I got released, there was a big 'Welcome Home' party for me and I got trashed. I didn't even last a night clean."

Dallas is staying with us for the weekend. It's the first time we've had him overnight. We've also invited him back for Thanksgiving and Christmas. On a run to the gas station I notice a photograph of Tristan and Maxim, my sons, taped to his dashboard. It's a shot of them making front double bicep poses on the beach in front of Torch Lake in Northern Michigan. We have become, in a way, his family—though we'll never replace his real family and don't want to, out of respect for them. Little things remind us that he still cares deeply for his brothers and still mourns his parents.

"I haven't celebrated the holidays in ten years," he says. "Both of my folks died in November, so I never feel much like celebrating."

As we ride along, his old Ford pickup rattling[8] around us, a Southern (the direction, not the denomination) Baptist preacher is screaming about "Jay-sus"[9] in the background. Actually, he's not screaming as much about Jaysus as he is about the evils of the bottle. An empty tape case reveals a sermon series from Pensacola Christian College, which is sort of the Magic Johnson of fundamentalist colleges, if Bob

8. The rear quarter panels are so eroded that they literally flap in the breeze as the truck makes its way down the highway.
9. This is Southern for Jesus.

Jones University is the Michael Jordan of such colleges in terms of fame and popularity.

It's been a long time since I've heard a sermon like this. There's a cadence to it. An emotional rising and falling of the proverbial tide. I've become accustomed to highly intellectual Reformed/neo-puritan sermons that sound more like college lectures with multiple points and outlines and Scripture references. The Jaysus guy is going right for our emotional jugular. He's speaking to our fears, except that instead of the Enemy (or our own sin nature) being the enemy, the enemy is beer. He spins out a narrative of a guy who, one night with his friends, says yes to one beer, which turns into a six-pack, which turns into a bottle of Vodka, which turns into a line of coke, which turns into prison. . . .[10]

The message here is that if the guy had just, somehow, avoided the beer in the first place, none of this bad stuff would have happened. He (Jaysus guy) is really passionate about this.

Dallas knows Jaysus guy is missing the point.

"It's important to flee temptation, to a degree," he says. "But it doesn't make you more spiritual, or bring any more glory to God, to just avoid everything. Women are a temptation, so should we just avoid women?"

Dallas used to date an exotic dancer. "She was really hot," he has said. We both acknowledge the power that hot women have over men. It never changes, and it's been this way since the beginning of time. This is made more difficult by the past that they shared before he was a believer. He's going to visit her tomorrow because he was close to her children. They called him Dad. He feels a certain responsibility for

10. It is strange to me that this qualifies as a "sermon." I think I've gotten spoiled (in a good way) by solid biblical teaching that happens verse by verse from Scripture.

her and for them, even though he knows she isn't any good for him and even though he's in a relationship—the first of his life—with a Christian woman. There's a part of me that wishes Dallas would just avoid his old girlfriend, but there's also a part of me (the right part, I think) that feels broken-hearted for her and wants Dallas to reach out to her. Still, this scares me to death.

He also admits that he's had a beer or three since he left for school.

"I had one one night right before I left," he says. "And twice since I've been up at school, I've gone into town and had one with dinner." I'm relieved and touched that he's told me. He's looking at me like he's expecting to hear what I think about it. Weirdly, even though Dallas is a recovering addict, I trust him in this area.

"You know how we approach it in our house," I explain. "You come over and see the occasional six-pack of beer or bottle of wine in our fridge. I like having one or two with dinner some nights, and I like having a glass of wine with Kristin. But I never get drunk, and I never use it to 'take the edge off' anything. I think you need to be careful how, when, and with whom you consume it, given your background. You're good now, but just make sure that when it hits the fan in life—and it will, whether it's a girl cheating on you or a job falling through or whatever—make sure you call me and don't try to take the edge off with booze." I hope I'm striking a good balance between the Jaysus guy and an "anything goes" friend. I trust Dallas. He's more mature than a lot of the mature people I know.

This is one of those Romans 14 situations where the act in question—moderate drinking—isn't expressly forbidden in Scripture, but I still want to make sure I'm properly caring for my weaker brother.

It's a topic that I know will come up again, as I know that recovering addicts are never really "out of the woods."

We're listening to Notorious B.I.G. while we lift weights. Biggie is singing about how he doesn't want "to go to heaven with the goodie-goodies" because "he likes black Tims[11] and black hoodies." It's great music to lift to, but a lot of the songs are about drinking and sex. And in a weird, but not at all surprising, theological turn,[12] some of the remixes that were recorded post-death by his collaborators are about how Biggie is in heaven now. Unless Biggie had a huge change of heart between these songs and his death, he's actually in hell, which should be more of a problem for us. But again, there's no better music to lift to. What we listen to, I realize, is another interesting Romans 14 situation.

There are no other lifters where Dallas goes to school. "They're all tools or nerds," he explains. I know exactly what he's talking about without him having to explain it (he does anyway). I know because I went to a Christian college. "There are rich kids in Abercrombie shirts and skinny jeans or kids who have never been out of their mom's living room." He feels out of place. It's strange that the fundies have tried so hard to whittle out the worldliness, but there's still a social strata in the world of Khakis and Golf Shirts (Walmart vs.

11. Timberlands, boots.

12. I say "not surprising" because it's been my experience that most people think their dead/dying loved ones are going to heaven because they were "good" people. However, if his songs were any indication, it's debatable as to how "good" Biggie was, and we know, as Christians, that it is not one's "goodness" that leads to eternal life. Rather, it takes an acceptance of the penalty that Christ paid on the cross for our sins. That is, it's more about what Christ did for us than about what we did/can do for Him.

Abercrombie and Hollister). I try to encourage Dallas by telling him that this never changes . . . it doesn't become different or better or easier with age.

Still, the other students, and even the staff at school, seem to have an unspoken respect for/fascination with Dallas. He's in a relationship with a girl from school which is, technically, against the rules. They're not calling it a relationship, but he texts her every five minutes and they spend hours on the phone at night.

"I get to bed around one or one-thirty every night," Dallas explains. "Lights-out is at eleven."

"What are you doing from eleven to one-thirty?" Kristin asks.

"Texting."

Kristin and I both really like this girl. Dallas brought her to our place to introduce us a few weeks ago. She was clever and a little bit sarcastic, and it was clear that she really cared for Dallas. She's the kind of person we would hang out with in real life, which made us all the more concerned when we learned that Dallas's plans to see his family in Ann Arbor fell through and he ended up spending the majority of the rest of the weekend with his ex-girlfriend the ex-stripper.

They met at a party when Dallas was eighteen. He was playing pool and explained that she was "the kind of girl who fed off the attention of other guys, so I knew exactly how to get through to her. I ignored her." It worked. She ended up on his lap on a sofa later in the evening, and the rest, as they say, is history. And by history I mean that even though their time together was relatively short, they shared a great deal both physically and emotionally. By his own admission, Dallas was "a mess" when they were together (see:

drugs, drinking, legal problems, etc.), but she "has a great mind and amazing potential," and he "loves her kids like they're [his] own." I also learn that she carried his child for a while—a pregnancy that ultimately and heartbreakingly ended in abortion, because she couldn't have a child with "a guy like him." I notice that his face goes dark, and he is near tears when he talks about it. "The kid would have been three this year," he says.

This is where the "friend" and the "mentor" in me butt heads as it pertains to the ex-girlfriend. The friend in me says, "Just trust his judgment, I'm sure nothing happened." (Translation: I hate confrontation and don't want to confront my friend.) But the mentor in me says that I need to say something. I listen, finally, to the mentor and craft the following email:

Hey Bro,

    I can't tell you how awesome it was to have you at our place Friday night. We all really enjoyed it, and my two boys adore you, man. It was really fun and relaxing to have you around.

    I'm writing tonight because sometimes I tend to over-communicate, and my mind is racing . . . so if this is one of those instances, please forgive me. A couple of things come to mind about your visit to our place, and then a couple of things about the rest of the weekend:

    1. I hope you always feel completely at home at our place . . . if you ever want to make long calls to your girlfriend, or just want to go out to the deck to smoke, you can always do that without feeling weird.

2. Kristin knows you smoke and is completely okay with that, so don't feel like you have to feel weird about that either.

As for the rest of the weekend:

1. The tickets[13] were awesome . . . thanks so much for thinking of us! Tris and I had an amazing time.

2. I trust you completely man . . . but especially given our conversation at Al's,[14] and your growing relationship with a Christian girl (which I think is great), I was surprised to hear that you'd spent the rest of the weekend w/ the dancer. This is one of those times where my gut reaction (being a people-pleaser, non-confronter) is to bury my head in the sand and just trust your wisdom and maturity. But it's eating at me a little—partly because I know how I would act if given twenty-four hours alone with an ex-stripper. That said, if you don't mind, just write or call tomorrow and put my mind at ease. I'm thinking not only of your integrity, but also what you're building relationship-wise and in life in general.

I hope that last part doesn't come off as just another older guy giving you a hard time. It's not intended to be that at all . . . I

---

13. Dallas was having a coffee at a downtown coffee shop when a guy known in the area as "The Turkey Man" entered, brandishing a wad of tickets for that afternoon's Michigan State vs. Minnesota football game. Dallas grabbed a couple for Tristan (my son) and me, and we had an amazing time. In case you're wondering, the guy is called "The Turkey Man" because he sells large turkey legs for fan consumption at Michigan State football games . . . making MSU perhaps the only major college stadium where you can randomly see fans walking around gnawing on turkey legs.

14. A super-cool cigar lounge in Lansing. Lots of oak paneling, leather sofas, and a huge-screen television.

consider you one of my closest friends. But I
want to make sure I take care of you as a mentor as well. I want to help you where I can,
and I don't want to drop the ball on that responsibility. If our friendship is nothing more
than lifting and working on cars, then I will
consider myself a failure in all of this.

Your Friend,

Ted

It's the next morning and I still haven't heard anything
from Dallas. However, half my mind is focused on our car—a
blue 1974 Triumph Spitfire. I laid eyes on the Spitfire the week
before in Grand Rapids and pretty much decided on the spot
that it was the perfect project for us. For one thing, the body
was in great shape . . . not much decay on the inside or out,
which tells me that it had been stored inside for most of its
life. It also had the requisite tough-looking wood grain and
black leather interior, not to mention chrome bumpers. It
was designed to look like a WWII fighter plane, after which
it was named.[15]

The previous owner, Brad,[16] had already started some work
on the guts of the Spitfire. He installed a new fuel line and
new filters and had replaced some hoses in the engine. He

15. The code name for this car was "The Bomb." It was designed by some
Italian guy with a cool-sounding name.
16. Brad looked like the kind of guy who could have totally ripped me off.
When I pulled up to his place, there were a bunch of cars sitting in various states
of repair in the driveway/lawn, suggesting that Brad was the kind of guy who
bought and sold cars like this often and could spot a sucker a mile away. But to
his credit, and to my appreciation, Brad didn't rip me off at all. In fact, I think he
gave me a pretty good deal.

also, it seems, left a bunch of random wires dangling out of the bottom of the dashboard. I don't ask him about this. It fired right up and ran while I looked at it, albeit with a lot of sputtering and coughing. It also died while I looked at it. Brad explained that the clutch needed work, and that the carburetors would have to be rebuilt. He opened the trunk to reveal an intimidating-looking pile of parts. Still, I'd seen enough.

I decided that afternoon to pull the trigger. This decision—to pull the trigger—was a little difficult for me, as are most decisions. I tend to dither over stuff like this. I justify and then re-justify before finally deciding.

"It's cheaper than a new MacBook Air," I said to my wife while dithering. "You don't have to justify it," she replied. "It's going to be a ton of fun in the summer," I continued. "You're going to look like Audrey Hepburn. We'll drive it on dates." She rolled her eyes some more. But I really did think about driving it on dates with her in the passenger's seat, wearing sunglasses and a scarf. I dream about driving it down a back road, parking, and making out.

This morning in my office I can think of little else but Dallas and the Spitfire. I'm wondering about the twenty-four hours that he spent away from school after he left my house. I'm hoping his integrity—and sobriety—remained intact.

The car rolls up on the back of a flatbed trailer, and I catch a glimpse of it out my office window. I grab Maxim (age four) and hustle out the front door to meet Brad, who arrives in a Range Rover hauling said-flatbed. I hadn't pegged Brad for a Range Rover kind of guy—if by a Range Rover kind of guy I mean a fiftyish CEO-type loaded to the gills with money. Brad is about my age, but he is neither CEOish or trust-fundish, meaning that his father probably financed the Rover. I'm probably over-thinking it.

We ease the little baby blue convertible off the trailer[17] (which gives me an appreciation for how truly tiny it is), and Brad sits behind the wheel, trying to coerce the engine into starting in the cold Michigan morning air. Finally, the motor springs to life and I take inventory of the interior. Sweet wood-grain dash. Check. Ripped black leather upholstery, which hopefully Kristin can mend. Check. Cool Sports Car Club of America medallion on dash. Check. We top off the clutch with brake fluid, and Brad gives me the job of sitting in the driver's seat, pumping the clutch. This will allow us to drive it around the block without grinding the gears and ruining the transmission.

Fast-forward an hour. Brad is gone, and I'm left with a brand-new old car sitting in my garage. I have the same feeling that I had when I was left alone with our boys for the first time. That sort of pit-of-the-stomach realization that this responsibility is mine. That said, there are going to be small victories and small defeats in this. I'm in this restoration for the long haul.

A short list of things that freak me out about this car:

- The ever-growing puddle of fluid on the floor of my garage, beneath the gearbox. This indicates that something is wrong with the clutch—something that will need to be dealt with as soon as possible if I ever want to drive this car farther than the end of my street.

---

17. I have this theory that everybody has a "sad jeans" story. Mine happened while we were trying to de-trailer the Triumph. I had on my favorite old pair of Levi's, which were already starting to tear around the back pockets, as old jeans are wont to do. As I was bending down, finessing the Triumph off the trailer, the whole backside of the jeans ripped out. Again, thanks to Brad for not saying anything about it or making me feel more like an idiot.

- The random box of parts that Brad left in the trunk. I recognize a couple of trim pieces, but there's lots of stuff I've never seen before. Yikes.
- The fact that when I toggled the light switch on the dash to the "on" position, smoke started billowing out of all of the dash's orifices. I quickly turned the light switch back to the "off" position and made a mental note to either a) take the dash apart and fix this, or b) only drive in the daytime. What sucked worse about this, and freaked me out more, was the fact that my wife was in the garage when I did this. I laughed it off and made some wisecrack about "the wiring in old cars," but truthfully I felt like an idiot.

Things I did right today:

- Successfully reattached, via screws, two pieces of cowling that fit alongside the steering column. These came out of the random box of parts in the back. Boom.
- Successfully reattached a piece of sweet dashboard wood-grain (out of which poured the aforementioned smoke) to the dash. Again, boom. Also took inventory of the rest of the random parts left in the trunk of the car. Trim pieces for rear quarter panels. Fuel additive. Brake fluid. An old radio. Worn-out particle board material that used to be a glove compartment. Oily rags.
- Learned the difference between the slave cylinder and the master cylinder in the clutch (thank you, Gary Strpko). In layman's terms, the master cylinder is the one you can see when you lift up the hood, and when you depress

the clutch you can see parts of it moving under a rubber covering. And it has a little reservoir into which goes the brake fluid, and which I can watch to see the level of the fluid lowering because there is a leak. I also learned that the slave cylinder[18] needs to be replaced, which is why it's leaking all over my garage floor.

- Also learned to identify the carburetor (thanks again, Gary). The car features dual Stromberg carbs, which are known for their high performance when they're working correctly. They're also known for not working correctly all that often. A little online research reveals that a Weber carb replacement kit for this car can be purchased for around three hundred bucks.

- Found out what a distributor cap is and learned that mine is shot.

- Successfully refilled the clutch reservoir with hydraulic fluid and learned that when it drains out, it fills with air, which means that it needs to be bled (i.e., have the air gotten out of it somehow). This (the bleeding) is a complicated process that involves taking, like, half the car apart, and it should probably just be done at whatever point we replace the slave cylinder.

When Gary comes over, he is completely complimentary and affirms me in my decision to buy the car, which feels good. It's good to have a car expert like him give the final sign-off on the purchase. We fire the engine and he skulks around the engine compartment, doing and looking at whatever it is that car guys do and look at.

18. It's a little three-inch metal cylinder into which the brake line is inserted and through which hydraulic fluid flows to the clutch.

"You'll need to get a nice legal pad and start making a list of what you need to do to get this thing road worthy," he says. "I would start with the clutch, and then think about replacing the carburetors." These old British convertibles are famous for their persnickety dual carbs, which require constant tinkering.

"And you'll want to look at a schematic[19] on this wiring," he says, remembering my smoke incident.

As I turn out the lights in the garage that night, I congratulate myself for being the kind of guy who has an old British convertible in his garage. I like the aesthetic of the thing. The lines are smooth and aggressive. The fact that the hood opens to the front also gives it a real race-car vibe. And I like that it's old. I like having connections to the past in my home. And, finally, I like that it makes my garage smell like "old car." I can do this.

---

19. Words I like: schematic. Though I've spent the majority of my life trying hard to avoid being the kind of guy who "looks at schematics."

5

I Don't Like People; I Like Dallas

Real men hide their emotions.

—Rocco, *Boondock Saints II: All Saints Day*

Let the peace of Christ rule in your hearts, since as members of one body you were called to peace. And be thankful. Let the word of Christ dwell among you richly as you teach and admonish one another with all wisdom, and as you sing psalms, hymns, and spiritual songs with gratitude in your hearts to God. And whatever you do, whether in word or deed, do it all in the name of the Lord Jesus, giving thanks to God the Father through him.

—Colossians 3:15–17

I was talking with my friend Cory today, telling him about Dallas and the amount of time we spend on the phone.

I've told Dallas to call anytime, day or night, and he's started to call me nearly every day.

"It's almost like you've got another kid," Cory said. "You must like people a lot more than I do."

"I don't like people," I responded. "I like Dallas."

Cory has been writing and preaching on discipleship, so naturally I've continued to use him as a sounding board for this project.

"*Disciple* is so churchy," he says. "The Greek word we translate as *disciple* basically means 'student.' But it's not a student like we carelessly use the term sometimes: a brain container with an ID number and a course checklist planted in a seat in front of a teacher who is trying to pour information into him and then test him on how much actually stuck. No, this kind of student is learning to be like his or her teacher (cf. Matt. 10:24–25[1]). There is a cognitive component to be sure, but thinking what the teacher thinks is just a means or a part of doing what the teacher does or living as the teacher lives.

"I think what I've just written is at the core of what Christian discipleship is," Cory continues, "but I don't think it fully describes it. And I have a feeling that we have assumptions about discipleship that are actually just contemporary ways of doing it that may be (and probably should be) adapted or discarded altogether."

I'm learning that discipleship has less to do with the books we read together and more to do with the kind of time and availability we give one another. That is, discipleship is highly relational, and while it often "works" within the confines

1. "The student is not above the teacher, nor a servant above his master. It is enough for students to be like their teachers, and servants like their masters. If the head of the house has been called Beelzebub, how much more the members of his household!"

of a set program, it's probably better if both parties *want* to communicate with one another. I'm not sure what Cory is talking about when he talks about ways of doing it that need to be discarded, but I'm guessing it has something to do with the awkward coffee meeting that inevitably starts with a question like, "So[2] . . . how are you doing . . . *spiritually?*" I hope I'm such good friends with my friends that I never have to start a conversation this way.

Like most college students his age, Dallas is up and down. The crisis with the dancer averted,[3] each day still brings a phone call, and with each phone call there is a wild fluctuation in mood. Today there is drama as to whether or not he'll even be able to afford a tank of gas to come down at Thanksgiving and work on the car.

"I'm tired of being broke," he says on the phone. I can tell within seconds whether he's in a good mood or a bad mood, and tonight he sounds completely dejected. The money in the Mission's fund is at a negative balance, and Dallas has no spending money at all. Still, I want to bring him down for Thanksgiving so he can spend the holiday with our family.

"I'm not real big on Thanksgiving," Dallas explains. "Both of my folks died in November. . . . I'm just not sure what I'm doing here (at school). I'm not sure where God wants me and what I'm going to do when it's over."

I pray silently that God would encourage Dallas and that he'd get what he needs to be able to come down for Thanksgiving.

The next evening Dallas calls, and there is more hope in his voice. "I got to share the gospel with a guy today," he says,

2. It's been my experience that sentences starting with the word *so* are almost always awkward . . . or a lie.
3. Dallas didn't stumble. He stood strong in the face of temptation.

and begins telling me a story of picking up a hitchhiker (yes, this freaks me out—see also: me being a wussy suburbanite) and then driving the guy to different churches, trying to get him some help.

"Dallas, I know the day-to-day is hard, but God really seems to be using you there. I thank God for this, man. You're getting to study, and you're getting to do ministry. That's what this year was all about."

I meet up with Dallas a few days later at the rescue mission, where he's speaking to the residents there. The Mission is nestled curiously in what may or may not be a gentrifying section of downtown. It's the kind of neighborhood that's trying to be cool but may not be there yet . . . and in fact the Mission may be what's keeping it uncool. Next to the Mission is a high-end salon, and around the corner is one of the more desirable restaurants in Lansing. Around the other corner is a piano bar, and across the street are the kinds of condos that upscale developers put together to try to lure people back into downtowns like these in blue-collar towns. For what it's worth, I think Lansing, Michigan, has the most vigilant parking-meter maids on the planet. Their vigilance may in fact be what's keeping downtown from becoming the kind of hip, upscale, "desirable" downtown that it wants to be. Or this could be me just being angry that I get a ticket seemingly every time I go downtown and am three minutes late to refill my parking meter.

Dallas was able to borrow money for a tank of gas from a classmate at school, and I'm thrilled that he'll be spending a few days with us. The Mission is bustling. It's the middle of the day, so they're doing a vigorous business serving lunch to Lansing's homeless. The clientele, all male, eye me warily. It's pouring outside, and I'm soaked from my walk from where I parked in front of the gentrified, desirable restaurant. "Is Dallas here?" I ask one of the men. "You done missed him," he replies before turning and walking away. Hmm.

I try the dining room, where I run into Rich, who runs the residential program at the Mission. He remembers me and greets me with a smile and a firm handshake. "How's work?" I ask him, making conversation. "Same old," he says. "Still fighting the battle . . . still on the front lines." I can't overstate how non-self-congratulatory he is when he says this. It's worth mentioning that a ministry like this attracts all kinds. Rich looks like he could take me apart with his hands. He's probably in his early forties and has a thick cop-mustache. I wouldn't mess with him. Mark, the executive director of the Mission, on the other hand, is smallish, with a kind face. Rich leads me upstairs where Dallas is leading a small-group discussion with all of the residential members of the Mission program. There are eight guys sprawled out on couches and chairs around a room that serves as a living room of sorts. There's a little kitchen with a fridge in the corner and a small bookshelf chock full of everything from solid theological tomes (I find books by John Piper and Mark Dever) to novels.

"I read most of these when I was in here," Dallas tells me later. "There wasn't a whole lot else to do." He shows me completed workbooks on anger management and weight loss. He shows me a non-functioning universal gym that is collecting dust in a corner. The whole room is, to be completely honest, almost unspeakably depressing. The kind of place you try hard to stay out of . . . although it has been a blessing in the lives of the men staying there. I can see bunk beds from where I'm sitting; they're practically on top of each other. There is a drippy institutional bathroom tucked away in a corner by a staircase. I can hear the dripping faucet from the living room. Dallas has told me many stories about the tension, conflict, and fights that happen here, and now I can see why. These guys are literally living on top of one another.

The men train their attention on Dallas as he speaks. "You're preparing for war when you get out of here," he says. He speaks slowly, deliberately, and humbly. He's dressed in a nice pair of jeans and a dress shirt. His shirtsleeves are rolled up to reveal arms covered with tattoos. He is the toughest-looking cat in a room full of tough-looking cats. There's a Hispanic kid in a hairnet—probably in his early twenties—and lots of guys who look to be middle aged. I talked to a guy who holds a PhD and used to be a lecturer at Oregon State University. He became a long-haul truck driver and then tried crack. There's a middle-aged guy across the room from me, sucking on a sucker, who was a high-level executive in an accounting firm before he tried and subsequently became enslaved to crack cocaine.

Crack is called crack[4] because it crackles when it's smoked. It made its first appearance in the inner cities of New York and L.A. in the mid-'80s, where it was introduced as a cheaper alternative to the real thing (coke). According to Wikipedia, crack cocaine is a substance that affects the brain chemistry of the user, causing euphoria, supreme confidence, loss of appetite, insomnia, alertness, increased energy, a craving

4. Other terms: rock, hard, iron, cavvy, or base.

for more cocaine, and potential paranoia (ending after use). Its initial effect is to release a large amount of dopamine, a brain chemical inducing feelings of euphoria. The high usually lasts from five to ten minutes, after which time the dopamine levels in the brain plummet, leaving the user feeling depressed and low. When cocaine is dissolved and injected, the absorption into the bloodstream is at least as rapid as the absorption of the drug that occurs when crack cocaine is smoked, and similar euphoria may be experienced. A typical response among users is to have another hit of the drug, but the levels of dopamine in the brain take a long time to replenish themselves, and each hit taken in rapid succession leads to increasingly less intense highs. However, a person might binge for three or more days without sleep, while partying with hits from the pipe.

According to the website crackreality.com, which was set up as a resource to help friends and loved ones deal with the crack addicts in their lives, "Crack cocaine makes people do bizarre and irrational things. You probably have seen some of them. If you try to make sense out of their actions, you will drive yourself crazy. Why would a person steal from their own family's home? Why would a straight man have sex with gay men? Why would a woman prostitute herself for $10 without using condoms? If you continually try to understand the 'whats' and 'whys' of the addiction, you will increase and prolong your emotional turmoil. Don't let that question, 'Why can't I understand?' reside in your mind. Everyone thinks they can help their addict. This is the furthest thing from reality. It is equivalent to thinking you can help a person beset by cancer. The difference is that attempting to help an addict only enables him to further his addiction. This is the most difficult concept to grasp. . . . For the moment just believe that 'understanding' and 'helping' are fruitless endeavors."[5]

The website goes on to explain that most crack addicts don't have jobs and can blow upwards of $200 to $400 a day on product as well as the food necessary to sustain life and the paraphernalia necessary to sustain the high. There is also the not-small issue of where to sleep and/or smoke crack. Every day the crack addict starts with no money and on many days no place to stay. According to the site, "These are resourceful, manipulative people who are able to create substantial amounts of cash daily." I can't do that. Even though the drive is completely sinful and misguided, the hustle is still impressive. Crack addicts will size up, manipulate, use, and discard the people in their lives. It's sobering (pardon the pun) to read this, and to realize that while Dallas is well on his road to recovery, relapse is still a very real possibility.

"I sold to cops, white-collar people, and even pastors when I was dealing," says Dallas. "You'd be surprised how many 'normal' people use this stuff." I am surprised. "I bet you were a good drug dealer," I reply, a little surprised to hear the words coming out of my mouth like that. What I mean is that the same things that make Dallas an effective communicator in this context—a sense of calm, listening skills, the ability to speak clearly, and a commanding voice—probably made him an exceedingly successful dealer. I ask him if he was ever nervous selling to cops. "Not really," he says. "You can tell a snitch from a mile away. They're always nervous. . . . They know that if they do or say something wrong, they could get killed."

5. http://crackreality.com/question.htm

Their stories are heartbreaking. "When people go back to the lifestyle (drugs), what they're really doing is escaping responsibility," Dallas says. "Life becomes too much to handle and they check out. Or they become institutionalized for life. I've seen guys within days of their parole get in fights or hit a guard just so they can stay in. Or guys will move from Mission to Mission just because it's easier than dealing with real life. They get used to the structure, the three meals a day, and the roof over their heads.

"If I can do this program, anyone can," Dallas continues to the group. "I was a mess when I got in here. I was angry. I didn't want to live. I wanted to punch Rich in the face." The men laugh as though the idea of punching Rich in the face has occurred to many of them. "You've got a new alarm system on the door because of me." Dallas smashed the alarm in a fit of rage.

"When you graduate this program," he says, "you're on to the real program.

"Being here helped me to realize that the staff aren't perfect . . . but they don't think they're perfect. They're here to guide us and give us good counsel."

"We want you to know Christ. That's all," adds director Mark Criss.

"Mark has been like a father to me," Dallas tells me later. I know that Mark and his wife have prayed, worried, and shed tears over Dallas this year. His heart for Dallas, and the rest of these men, is an unbelievable example to me.

Over Mark's shoulder is a painting that Dallas did while he was in the Mission. It's a depiction of the seven woes appearing in Matthew 23, which deal almost exclusively with the Pharisees and hypocrisy. Being true to oneself is important to

Dallas and to the other guys in the Mission. It's a tension that makes doing life outside the Mission walls especially difficult.

"You have a hedge of protection around you here," Dallas says. "I still have unbelieving friends and family out there, and I love them, but I can't surround myself with them on a daily basis. You're replacing that old life with something that is even greater. . . . Nothing in your old life can compare with the joy and peace that comes from Christ."

Mark is called to the kitchen, but he asks me to read from 2 Peter 1, verses 3–10:

> His divine power has given us everything we need for life and godliness through our knowledge of him who called us by his own glory and goodness. Through these he has given us his very great and precious promises, so that through them you may participate in the divine nature and escape the corruption in the world caused by evil desires.
>
> For this very reason, make every effort to add to your faith goodness; and to goodness, knowledge; and to knowledge, self-control; and to self-control, perseverance; and to perseverance, godliness; and to godliness, brotherly kindness; and to brotherly kindness, love. For if you possess these qualities in increasing measure, they will keep you from being ineffective and unproductive in your knowledge of our Lord Jesus Christ. But if anyone does not have them, he is nearsighted and blind, and has forgotten that he has been cleansed from his past sins.
>
> Therefore, my brothers, be all the more eager to make your calling and election sure. For if you do these things, you will never fall.

The words sound like they were written for these men, and for all of us. There's so much in this passage, but what jumps out immediately is the desire of these men to escape the corruption in the world caused by evil desires. And Dallas is quick to point out that graduation from the program doesn't mean the cessation of these desires. "I still have a desire to do it sometimes . . . to go back to the old way of living. I see a pretty girl walking down the street and I still think about what I would have done."

———

The men really benefitted from Dallas's talk, and all expressed a desire to see him again. Everyone in the program—from Mark to Rich to the guys—seems to want to be reminded that it can work. Dallas is that reminder.

He's still a young kid. I'm reminded of this as he limps down the stairs on the way to our lunch meeting. His arms are both skinned raw.

"So what happened to you?" I ask.

"I was wrestling with this kid at school on the carpet—he's about three hundred pounds—and I separated my shoulder," he says. "I got pulled over driving home from the hospital because I was shifting with my left hand and weaving all over the place. The cop was laughing at me, but he let me go without a ticket."

I breathe an audible sigh of relief.

———

When Dallas first lays eyes on the car, I can tell he's in his element. His movements around the car and underneath the hood are like a panther bounding over the rocks. Put simply, he knows what he's doing in this context. My garage, on the other hand, is lacking a certain . . . *atmosphere*. My kids' sleds and bicycles hang on the walls, and there is an assortment of toys strewn about. Definitely not what I remember Gramps's garage looking like; his was like a shrine to manhood, with a workbench, a fridge, ashtrays, Schlitz calendars, and all manner of tools lying around. I'll need to work on this.

"These engines are so simple to work on," Dallas says, staring at the mass of steel and wires. It looks unspeakably complicated to me. We unscrew a broken cooling fan that is stuck to the front of the engine and take it to an auto-parts store in search of a replacement. It's a long shot, but perhaps these small fans are semi-standard. The young guy at the auto-parts store is intrigued by our project. "I've been playing Gran Turismo IV on the Playstation 2,"[6] he explains, "and I always use the '74 Triumph." I take this as a small compliment and affirmation of my choice. Unfortunately, the fan is going to run us $61 plus shipping and is only available from an outfit named Victoria British, with whom we'll end up doing a lot of business on this project. They specialize in rare, and therefore humorously expensive, British auto parts. The auto-parts store itself is a revelation. I've always avoided these places like the plague and actually can't tell you the last time I've been in one. He gives me the lay of the land, so to speak, and we have our eye on a metric socket kit that will allow us to do a lot of our engine repair. It doesn't even have a price tag. This worries me.

We leave with a can of starter fluid (cost: $2.99—a victory!), as Dallas is determined to get the motor running tonight. Before we left, it sputtered and coughed and made a distinctively sick sound, which made us think we'd thrown a rod.[7] When we arrive at the garage, Dallas puts on reading

6. For my older readers: This is a video game.
7. This is bad. It happens deep inside the engine and would have required us to basically take the entire top part off the engine, take apart the pistons, and then find the bad rod. This would have taken forever.

glasses, resulting in an oddly professorial look, and begins to take apart the carburetors. We assumed we'd be replacing the notoriously junky twin-carbs with an American-style upgrade kit, but Dallas hypothesizes that shot air filters may be the cause of our sputtering engine. He removes the filters and sprays a little bit of fluid directly into the carbs themselves. He also essentially hot-wires the car from the engine compartment so that he can ignite and throttle the engine manually. His previous career[8] is paying dividends.

I have been here at school for almost four months now, and every day has been a struggle. I am engulfed in a culture that is foreign to anything I have ever experienced before. Judgments, false assumptions, and shallowness run high, which makes it difficult to focus on the goals that have brought me here. I stand out like a sore thumb. Most of the people here are home-schooled kids who grew up in good Christian homes; I definitely don't fit that criteria. I'm a big guy covered in tattoos and grew up in the definition of a dysfunctional home. It's hard to relate to people here, since we're on opposite ends of the social spectrum.

But the truth of the Bible rings true as always. Our Lord makes a promise in Proverbs 16:7, saying, "When a man's ways please the LORD, he makes even his enemies to be at peace with him." I am not saying these people are my enemies, but I am saying that it is my duty to live a life that is pleasing to God, and He will handle these issues in His own time and way. I find comfort in this because it motivates me to persevere during this ongoing trial, and it prevents me from beating people to a pulp for treating me like the new exhibit at the zoo. God has placed

8. Dallas used to steal cars.

me here for a reason, so I am not going to get discouraged and give up on the hard work that I have already invested by being here just because people want to gossip. I can't be too harsh in my judgments of the people here either. I realize they are only human and have their own struggles as well.

As bad as things may seem at times, I really am thankful to be here because I have learned many valuable truths through my experiences. One of these truths is that people don't always see the bigger picture; they are bound to their own paradigms of the truth. Perspective is a difficult issue in life; when we don't have all the facts, we often form conclusions that aren't true. This is something that we all need to work on by patiently gathering facts before we come to hasty conclusions. We don't always see things as clearly as we think.

This has been an extremely humbling time in my life, because I have had to constantly evaluate myself and bring my shortcomings to the Lord as well as apply biblical truths to my relationships (which will be an ongoing process until I die). One of these biblical truths again comes from the book of Proverbs. Verse 15:1 says, "A gentle answer turns away wrath, but a harsh word stirs up anger." I have been an extremely violent and angry person in the past, and during times of confrontation and accusation it is hard to hold back from backsliding into my previous methods of handling problems. I have had to rely completely on the strength of the Holy Spirit and remember this truth during these times. This doesn't mean that I just lie down and let people say anything they want to me without standing up for myself; it simply means I remain calm and voice my side of things, standing up for what I know to be true in a way that honors God. I'm not perfect (obviously). I have had moments where I have acted on impulse and torn into people without thinking, but this exhortation from God has prevented me from doing that on a regular basis and then living in regret. Also, I have to keep in mind that

I'm already on probation for an assault that happened before my salvation.

I have to look at this experience as a training ground for a greater, ongoing spiritual war that I will inevitably face outside of this Christian sub-culture. The things that I'm facing here are going to be magnified tenfold when I step back into the secular world. So like any good soldier, I'm learning from this training ground and girding myself up for the battles I'll face in the future. We need to be prepared for adversity. The only way we can do this is by learning from our experiences, putting on the whole armor of God, and relying on God's strength and wisdom to help us persevere.

When I came to this Christian college, I had unrealistic expectations of what this experience would be like. I now realize that no matter where you go, you will face circumstances and relationships that aren't perfect, even in Christian circles. We often put Christian culture on a pedestal and expect perfection. In reality, Christians have to face the same struggles the rest of the world does; we're just supposed to handle them differently, and we have a holy God to help guide us through. Even though we should look different than the world in action and speech, expecting perfection is unrealistic. I continue to grow in my walk with God and fellow Christians, but during this time I have realized that it takes great effort to make that happen. You have to be a friend in order to have friends. I have had to remind myself of these truths every day and put forth the effort to be the man that God wants me to be.

6

Black Tims and Black Hoodies

On Drugs, Rage, and False Gods

It's true I have a lot of friends in politics, but they wouldn't be so friendly if they knew my business was drugs instead of gambling which they consider a harmless vice. But drugs, that's a dirty business.

—Don Corleone, *The Godfather*

It is not a true Gospel that gives us the impression that the Christian life is easy, and that there are no problems to be faced. That is not the New Testament teaching. The New Testament is most alarming at first, indeed terrifying, as it shows us the problems by which we are confronted. But follow it—go on! It does not stop halfway, it goes on to this addition, this second half; and here it shows us the way in which, though that is the truth concerning the battle, we can be enabled to wage it, and not only to wage it, but to triumph in it. It shows us that we are meant to be "more than conquerors."

—D. Martyn Lloyd-Jones, *Spiritual Depression*

Hey, bro, I'm about to break a guy's jaw up here. . . . I just need to talk for a minute." I can tell from the tone of Dallas's voice that he's almost out of control. What's most important is to keep him on the phone, reasoning that at least if he's holding a cell phone and talking to me, he can't punch another guy in the face.

What's weird is that the call comes at the exact moment that many of our friends are arriving at our house for a small group Bible study—the same Bible study that Dallas used to be a part of. Through the French doors in my office I can hear the pleasant voices of Christian suburbanites greeting each other, being offered snacks, and generally feeling jovial. I wish I could be a part of it, but I'm glad Dallas has confided in me, because things are reaching critical mass at the conservative Bible school.

What I can gather is this: Dallas had a semi-productive meeting with an administrator over some disciplinary issues, namely his "attitude" and his relationship with a girl up there. They reached what I thought was an understanding. Then the next morning Dallas received a letter laying out the new parameters of his discipline—namely no contact of any kind with this girl—and stormed into the administrator's office to have it out. After a shouting match, Dallas slammed the door and left . . . and called me. (I thank God for that.)

Visions of Dallas getting kicked out of school and ending up on my doorstep are running through my mind. Over the phone I preach the same things to him I have before—self-control, thinking about the long-term, etc. He knows the right answers because he's an intelligent kid, so I mostly just let him talk. I am also mentally game-planning my phone call to the administrator. Dallas gives me the guy's number, and I promise to call him as soon as I get off the phone. My stomach is doing flip-flops because I hate confrontation more than pretty much anything on earth. Before I let him go, I reinforce to Dallas that he needs to stay sober tonight and not do anything stupid, and that not getting kicked out of school is of paramount importance. We need to have something to show for this crazy experience. I tell him that at the very least he's getting three square meals a day and a roof over his head. It occurs to me that this is what people say about prison. I tell him I love him.

I dial the administrator's number.

"Hey, buddy," he says when he picks up the phone. Buddy? I realize this is probably standard youth pastor talk. I choose to overlook it, even though the guy and I are not buddies. I can tell right away that he's stressed out and still buzzing from the fight-or-flight response that he just experienced vis-à-vis my tattooed ex-con buddy nearly caving his face in. I don't blame him for that at all. Any sane human being would have been scared out of his mind.

He tells me that Dallas stormed out of his office and "slammed the door in my face." He tells me that Dallas's spirit was "anything but repentant and teachable," and then tells me that they're considering sending him packing. I tell him that that doesn't sound like the Dallas I know and that I just spoke with him and that we're both committed to him finishing the year with a teachable heart. I also admit to him that I don't understand many of the rules they have in place, but that I am committed to Dallas following them to the best of his abilities, since he had committed to doing that.

To his credit, the guy is cool about it. "It" being my lack of understanding of why or how wearing a shirt and tie all over the place and listening to bad music makes you somehow more spiritually grounded than people who do things like have a television and read mainstream books. The fundamentalist ethic seems to be that it's possible for a person to avoid temptation entirely, and therein lies the secret to a healthy spiritual life. My desire for Dallas is that through Scripture, prayer, and growth in Christ, he would have the necessary tools to fight temptation, knowing that he can't spend the rest of his life sequestered in a never-ending church camp environment, much less getting through the year without committing administrator-cide. The guy also seems to think that this girl Dallas is seeing is "bringing him down." I comment that that may be a possibility, but then I ask him if he remembers what it's like to be twenty-two and madly in love with someone. There is silence on the other end of the line.

I reassure him that it wasn't, and isn't, my desire to undermine his authority—rather, it's just that I'm the only person Dallas has to call. I explain to him that if another, more "normal" student had a discipline problem, they would call their mom and dad to receive counsel and talk it out, and that in this scenario, I'm playing that role for Dallas. The whole vibe of the conversation is positive, and we agree to approach this thing together. Except for the small detail that Dallas has left campus and nobody knows where he went. We agree to talk again when everybody can gather around a speaker phone later in the evening. I hang up, praying that Dallas is safe and making wise choices and that the Lord would guide him back to campus safely with a repentant spirit. The rules may be wrong, but it was even more wrong for him to disrespect the administrator. And it was a breach of what I call the Free Agent Plan.

The Free Agent Plan is something I came up with one time when I was talking to Dallas about his life. The terminology comes from sports (which is my world) and refers to the fact that everything you do on the field either raises or lowers your "stock" in the eyes of your team and other teams. This means that when you sign your next contract, all of this stuff factors in. I have been trying to communicate to Dallas that he is a free agent in life—and that everything he does, good or bad, either raises or lowers his stock. This affects his ability to get and keep jobs, meet decent girls, etc. For example, handling a challenging situation with class and dignity = raised stock. Making out with a stripper from your past = lowered stock. And so forth. This, of course, is nothing earth shattering and is just common sense, but when emotions (read: sins) like anger and lust enter the picture, common sense often goes out the window. I know this from experience.

It also occurs to me that Dallas is no stranger to dealing with institutions and authority. However, in the past I think he's used his exemplary communication skills and natural charm to bend situations to his benefit. I've heard from others that when he was in lockup[1] he "ran the place" and had much older, much more hardened criminals deferring to his authority. This is a testimony to his charisma, but also to the fact that breaking jaws to get respect was a way of life in places like that.

---

1. In fact, when Dallas talks about lockup, he talks about how he had "way more freedom" inside than he does at the fundamentalist school.

I hang up the phone and slink out into our small group meeting, exhausted. All this conflict resolution has taken it out of me. I find a spot on the floor by the fireplace, and we all take a moment to pray for Dallas.

Later, the phone rings again. Dallas is back on campus and sitting in the office. I greet him on the speaker phone (aside: I hate speaker phones—everyone gets weird), and we start talking about solutions. "We're thinking of letting Dallas come down there tonight," says the administrator. "He needs to clear his head and prepare himself to come back with a different spirit." I wholeheartedly agree, if for no other reason than to get him out of there, which is going to be best for everyone's health. He agrees to spend the night on campus and then come to us the following morning. "I'm not gonna be able to sleep here," he says. I tell him that the roads are too bad because of the weather, and it's too late at night for him to come. "I've had many sleepless nights," I hear myself telling him. "Use the time to pray, think, read, or just enjoy the quiet." I sound exactly like my parents. I tell him I love him, hang up, and then collapse onto our bed.

"It feels like we've got a twenty-two-year-old kid," I tell Kristin. One complicating factor is the fact that Dallas literally can't afford to come down to see us without some miraculous financial intervention. Bills and cost of living have eaten up his meager cash reserves, and he has nothing left with which to fill his gas tank tomorrow. Before he hangs up we resolve to pray about it, which we do.

The next morning our advance checks for this project arrive in the mail. Praise God.

We spend the following day making preparations to have Dallas. Every time I walk past the car in the garage, I get warm, excited feelings, remembering the work we've done up to this point and excited to get under the hood again. On tap for this week is to remove, take apart, and completely clean the carburetors, in hopes that it improves the car's performance and takes the choppiness out of the way the engine runs.

We've got a previously scheduled dinner party at the house, but I've invited Dallas and assured him that it's okay. I expect him to arrive any minute, and check my phone often through the dinner. I receive a text around nine-thirty, telling me that he's decided to spend the night in Ann Arbor with his grandparents.

This fills me with renewed worry because Ann Arbor is the site of many of his mistakes in the past. Ann Arbor proper, i.e., the home of the University of Michigan, is sort of like one giant Starbucks full of affluent/outwardly-thoughtful-activist types who wear North Face jackets and pontificate and do yoga and are into causes. But a few miles away is Ypsilanti, where Dallas spent much of his growing-up years. Ypsi, as it's affectionately known, is seedy and rough—lots of gang activity, crack houses, hubcap joints, and liquor stores. On its best day it's still depressing. Hence the worry.

I try to get Dallas to come to town, but he refuses. I try to get him to come to a church Christmas party, but he turns that down too. "I don't feel much like a bunch of chitchat tonight," he says, which I totally understand, but I still wish he was where I could see him, and where I knew he'd be safe.

When Dallas finally arrives I learn a lot more about Ann Arbor. I learn that while he's there, he spends most of his time with his friend Marcus, who is sober and gainfully employed, which relaxes me considerably. What's more, by the way Dallas talks about him, I can tell that he is fiercely loyal to Marcus and needs to see him. I will have to trust God to finish the good work He started in Dallas, and allow him to re-engage, to a certain degree, with his life in Ann Arbor. Still, this scares me to death.

I also learn a lot more about carburetors. Our job today, as mentioned, is to completely disassemble, clean, and rebuild our dual Stromberg carbs, on the chance that doing so will improve their performance and improve the performance of the engine. It's cold—Michigan winter cold—in the garage, so we haul up the portable heater from the basement, run to the auto-parts store[2] to buy gloves, and start working.

The carburetors are themselves two pieces, and those two pieces are comprised of two pieces. There's a piston that goes up and down, controlling the flow of air through the engine, and then, technically speaking, the bigger part underneath, where the gasoline goes. When that piston gets gunked over, it doesn't work right. The engine either gets too much or too little air, resulting in the rough—or in our case nonexistent—idle, and the roughness in running. Remove the gunk, the logic goes, and improve the engine's performance.

Aside: We spend the first hour of the morning trying to get the engine to fire and turn over. This has happened pretty easily in the past, but it's tough going today. Dallas continues to ply the carbs with starting fluid, and I continue to push-button start the engine to no avail. Dallas is perplexed, and

2. I'm becoming semi-comfortable in here, which is semi-miraculous. I feel like they don't immediately know I'm a poseur as soon as I walk in the door. Note: They still know this at the used-record store and the skate shop.

he's checking and re-checking connections. I finally offer the following: "You know, Dallas, this gas gauge doesn't work. . . . I wonder if we're out of gas?" I grab a yardstick and stick it in the tiny gas tank, which is immediately behind the driver's seat. Sure enough, it's bone dry. We sheepishly admit defeat and fill up a gallon container at the gas station down the street, happy there's nothing seriously wrong with the motor.

Once we fill the tank, we fire the engine and assess the gunked-up carbs. Soon they are in pieces on a shop blanket, and we're spraying them with an agent that is supposed to de-gunk them. While the agent is working, Dallas hauls his laptop out to the garage and cues up some music for me—Five Finger Death Punch. "This stuff really communicates a lot of what I'm feeling right now," he says, cuing up a song called "The Bleeding."

"I pretty much learned how to do all this stuff by watching my dad," he says while gently de-gunking the carburetor with a shop rag. I've seen pictures of Dallas's dad; he pretty much looked like an older version of Dallas. A big, tough hombre.

"I got moved up to head maintenance manager at the truck stop because I knew how to do this. They used to send this kind of thing out." Dallas got a job in a truck stop sandwich shop right after his release from lockup. Soon he was helping truckers fix their engines, and working his way up the food chain.

"Did you and your dad do a lot of projects like this?" he asks.

"We did a lot together," I tell him, "but nothing like this. We lifted, ran, went to ballgames, and talked together a ton, but stuff like this was a little out of our depth. We were both intimidated by these kinds of projects, so we never did them. But I think the important thing was the time we spent together."

"My dad busted my [chops][3] a lot while doing this stuff," he says. "His way of saying he loved me was making fun of me, I think." He says this with a laugh. Dallas's father was a long-haul truck driver; he was away for long stretches of time. He battled his own addictions. "I don't want to make him the bad guy in all of this," Dallas says.

The carbs clean, we begin the process of reassembly. The screws and pieces are neatly archived in the little plastic containers that come with lunchmeat. (I've found that these are perfect for storing small parts.) Once assembled, the engine roars to life. We win.

"Let me be clear about this. I don't have a drug problem. I have a police problem."

—Keith Richards, The Rolling Stones

Everywhere I go, it seems, I'm reminded of Dallas. I'm sitting in a darkened movie theatre with a friend, watching *The Fighter*.

It's probably clear by now that I love boxing. I used to love covering the sport as a writer. Like most fight fans, I remember Irish Micky Ward from his megabattles with Arturo Gatti in the early 2000s. I never got to cover those fights, but I wished I had because they represented everything that is great about boxing—courage, valor, talent, and two guys who absolutely

---

3. Publisher-friendly terminology. Dallas's word was different.

refused to quit taking each other's beatings—but also who became genuine friends outside the ring after their battles. Ward was Irish and Gatti was Italian . . . which added even more to the old-school/throwback/warrior ethos they both cultivated.

The Fighter is a movie that you might not be interested in if you're not a boxing fan, but it's really a film about family and relationships, and it's just masquerading as a boxing film (although the boxing part is good too). It stars Mark Wahlberg—who I still and will always call Marky Mark, as Ward, but it has nothing to do with the Gatti fights, which happened during the twilight of Ward's career. It has everything to do with family, obligation, drugs, friendship, small towns, and dreams. It co-stars Christian Bale, who is famous for being Hollywood's current petulant/temperamental/super-talented male actor. He is absolutely, lights-out ridiculous[4] as Dicky Ecklund, Ward's older brother who is also a fighter, plus Ward's trainer and a crack addict.

Reasons I love *The Fighter*:

1. The soundtrack. There's a scene before Ward's title fight at the end where he and Dicky are in the tunnel, ready to walk to the ring, with their heads together listening to "Here I Go Again" by Whitesnake. This scene is worth the price of admission. The movie features a ton of other great '80s rock songs as well.
2. Bale is creepy-good as the charismatic crack addict Ecklund. Ecklund was known as "The Pride of Lowell, Mass.," because of his performance vs. Sugar Ray Leonard and, given the reactions of people as he walked/

4. In a good way. This is my version of "sick."

jogged the streets, he seemed to be the de facto mayor of Lowell. Everybody loved him, but he had a serious self-destructive bent, which Bale captured perfectly. He showed the inherent lovability of a person who still had serious character flaws. This struck me as very real.

3. Amy Adams was amazing as Ward's girlfriend. She was a barkeep, a college dropout, and maybe the reason Ward got his career on track and was able to secure meaningful big-money fights late in his career.

4. The family dynamics. Ward had a domineering mother/manager, an older brother he idolized (Ecklund) but who may have been ruining his career, and a bunch of half-crazy siblings (with half-crazy '90s hairdos) to whom he felt obligated. He felt the weight of his family and their well-being/happiness on his shoulders at all times. This film does an unbelievable job portraying this.

5. The boxing. The film is boxing heavy at the beginning and at the end . . . and the boxing is believable and inspiring. It made me want to immediately go to my basement and shadowbox in the ring. It also does this cool thing where the boxing scenes in the film are made to look like old '90s videotape from ESPN and HBO.

6. The redemptive note that it strikes at the end.

Caveat: Being that the film is set in blue-collar Boston and is about boxing, well over half of the sentences in the movie feature the F word. Just thought I should warn you.

There are these arresting scenes of Ecklund smoking crack out of a makeshift pipe, fashioned from an empty two-liter bottle. And more arresting than the actual scenes of the smoking are the scenes that portray Ecklund's animal-like desire for more crack—such that he breaks huge commitments (like his brother's fight in Atlantic City) and repeatedly breaks his mother's heart. Each time Ecklund's mother comes to the door of his crack house, he scurries to a back window and jumps down two stories into a Dumpster full of garbage, which seems fitting. What's odd is that people in the theatre laugh at this . . . though I find it to be one of the saddest things I've ever seen on screen.

I know that these are all things Dallas experienced. There's another scene where Ecklund is alone in his jail cell—wearing a jumpsuit, with the automatic door of the cell closing behind him—and he is curled up on his cot, screaming and sweating as the throes of crack withdrawal overtake him. I know that this is how Dallas detoxed—cold turkey in a cell—because he told me. It seems like the most lonely, isolating, hopeless, heartbreaking thing imaginable.

I'm reminded that it is out of this despair that the Lord plucked Dallas. In His sovereignty He chose my friend for glory. The thought of that brings tears to my eyes. There's something very powerful to me about seeing a visual portrayal of what Dallas went through as a way to further appreciate the work that God did on his behalf. The thing about discipleship is that it feels at times like a constant barrage of hard work—there is always another phone call or meeting or crisis to manage. But at the end of the day, I'm thankful to *The Fighter* for reminding me what Christ did for sinners like me. And I'm thankful for my friend, for his sobriety, and for the fact that he knows God.

In an attempt to further understand Dallas's background and situation, I buy a book called *Hero of the Underground:*

My Journey Down to Heroin and Back, by Jason Peter. It initially caught my attention because Peter was one of the football players I watched from afar during my formative high school and college years. When I was in high school, he was at Nebraska, and I idolized his huge muscles and shaved-headed warrior mentality. In short, he was a tough-guy's tough guy, and I wanted to be him.

The book chronicles Peter's ascension to football glory—from a prep school in New Jersey to the Nebraska Cornhuskers, where he was an All-American defensive tackle and eventually a first-round draft choice. Nebraska is also where he had his first pain pill—an attempt to ward off the aches brought on by playing football at a high level. Heavy drinking, pain pills, cocaine, crack, and finally heroin would become a daily, hourly way of life for Peter.

What it is, really, is a book about worship. It's about the sensation that Peter felt as an elite athlete, as 75,000 rabid Nebraska fans screamed his name every afternoon for four years. He describes this process beautifully. As an ex-athlete myself, it gives me chills. What Peter was describing was his own process of becoming a god and how intoxicating that was for him. When he went to the NFL—to an indifferent town (Charlotte, North Carolina), where wins and real friendships were scarce—he began to fill the void with substances. Local doctors, all too happy to dispense pain meds in exchange for jerseys and face time with famous athletes, were easy marks . . . and soon Peter was on to the harder drugs that would control his life.

Put simply, Peter wanted something that would get close to replicating the buzz he felt as a dominant, elite athlete, where week in and week out he was challenging and vanquishing the best the world had to offer. Quite frankly, life without that feeling just wasn't doing it for him. He needed something that would replicate the feeling of being worshiped. Except that as believers, we know man wasn't created to be worshiped but to worship our Creator. This presented something of a problem for Peter, who is adamant about his unbelief throughout the book. Still, he writes incredible prose about the use, and detox from, hard drugs:

> Doctors will tell you that kicking heroin is like having a severe flu . . . well, as any addict can tell you, doctors—for all of their good intentions—really don't know (expletive). Comparing heroin withdrawals to the flu is like comparing getting hit by a truck to falling off a tricycle. I don't care how severe your flu is, it's unlikely that you've seriously considered throwing yourself out a window just to make the screaming in your head go away and the agony in your body stop. Heroin is the nearest thing to hell that the living ever get to experience.

If the definition of idolatry is worshiping created things rather than the Creator, then drug use is the epitome of idolatry. Peter writes the way Dallas speaks—of the consuming nature of drugs, and of the fact that it becomes the altar at which you worship 24/7.

I asked celebrity pastor/author C. J. Mahaney about this once, as we were driving around Lansing on the way to the airport. I asked him about the spiritual implications of drugs—that is their right/wrongness in relationship to something like alcohol, which we seem to be able to do in moderation. "Drugs open up the user to specific spiritual challenges," says Mahaney, himself a former drug user, meaning that while it is possible to use alcohol in moderation, Mahaney would argue

103

(at least from experience) that he was unable to do the same thing with marijuana. Marijuana became, for him, a god.

Jason Peter writes,

> All I had now were the pills. Gradually there was no pretense anymore that their primary use was pain control. They were just another way to stop me from feeling. I was taking up to eighty Vicodin ES a day. . . . I would swallow them by the handful or grind them up to snort. Nothing could ever get me where I wanted to go. Total oblivion was the goal.

I can relate to that goal; it is the promise of total oblivion that makes controlled substances so completely attractive, especially when compared to knowing a Lord who doesn't offer ease and a primrose path in exchange for our loyalty.

7

These Boyish Good Looks

In this country, you gotta make the money first. Then when you get the money, you get the power. Then when you get the power, then you get the women.

—Tony Montana, *Scarface*

Johnny Cash writes that sooner or later, God will cut you down. But I've found that He often does so through women. I can tell from his Facebook statuses that Dallas is having woman troubles. His statuses read like Bad English lyrics from the late '80s—they're all about love and loss and heartbreak and passion and bleeding and all that. I send him the following message:

```
Hey Bro,
    I saw your Facebook status and can tell that
you're in the throes of some serious heart-
mashing love with (name omitted). I recognize
```

this because I've been there before. Ahh . . .
I've got some long stories and stuff I need to
tell you sometime, man. Remind me when we're in
person.

Anyway, all that to say I know how you feel
and I know the roller coaster you're on—where
your emotions can change from text to text, from
phone call to phone call. Where you're reading
the inflections in her voice . . . the things she
says . . . and it determines how you feel about
yourself, about God, and about the future.

My advice to you is this—keep doing what
you're doing, which is going all in with your
heart. Every good man loses his heart at least
once to a woman he can't have. This is part of
your formation as a man . . . and it takes guts
to put yourself out there like that. I admire
that. But the second part of my advice is to
not let her take your mind. You need to keep
making decisions in a rational, calculated way,
because you have an unbelievable mind (a gift)
and an amazing future ahead of you. Getting to
that future involves not letting anyone or anything dictate your emotions (and subsequently
your actions).

Anyway, man, I like her and she could be the
one . . . only the Lord knows that (and then
the two of you). And I'll support you in everything as it pertains to her. Hang in there.

Ted

I think Facebook is a mixed blessing. I'm realizing that I'm
finding out a lot about Dallas's emotions via his Facebook

page. Facebook pages are very public, very exhibitionistic places to process things. Most statuses are innocuous ("I'm making a sandwich," "I got a new iPhone") or have some thinly veiled agenda like showing the world how spiritual or intelligent you are. Dallas's are increasingly emo[1] with regard to his relationship, which strikes me as surprising coming from someone as grizzled and seemingly old-school as Dallas.

My wife and I are realizing that we met and fell in love in the relative dark ages, before email was huge, and certainly before social networking was a glimmer in anyone's eye. When I was love-sick or full of rage, I would throw a Pantera tape into my Walkman and lift weights, or I would spend a sleepless night pacing a hole in the carpet. Now, because of the miracle of Facebook, you can share those emotions with the world.

What's weird is that Dallas posted those statuses for the world (or at least his ex-girlfriend) to see, but when I reached out to him and asked him about them, he said he didn't want to talk about it. I feel like I'm losing him, to a certain degree. The phone calls are fewer and farther between, and lower in quality. I feel like he's being pulled in, deeper and deeper, by influences from his "old life." I'm wondering about his sobriety, cognizant of the fact that nothing very productive happens in the wee hours of the morning (the Facebook statuses in question were posted at 4:00 a.m.). I take comfort in the fact that Dallas's conversion was real, and that He belongs to the Lord, and that the Lord will finish the good work He

1. *Emo* is short for emotional. The shortened version of the word has come to represent both a personal style aesthetic (mopey, morose) and a genre of music (also mopey, morose).

began in my friend. I'm also convinced that getting there is going to be a wild ride.

I'm reading in Lamentations 3, and I'm comforted by the wild swings of emotion that mark the text—the absolute crushing, dark, terrifying feeling of loneliness and pain, but also the author's steadfast belief in God's goodness, even in the midst of God's discipline. And even in the midst of the feeling that God is distant.

> I am the man who has seen affliction
> by the rod of his wrath.
> He has driven me away and made me walk
> in darkness rather than light;
> indeed, he has turned his hand against me
> again and again, all day long.
>
> He has made my skin and my flesh grow old
> and has broken my bones.
> He has besieged me and surrounded me
> with bitterness and hardship.
> He has made me dwell in darkness
> like those long dead.
>
> He has walled me in so I cannot escape;
> he has weighed me down with chains.
> Even when I call out or cry for help,
> he shuts out my prayer.
> He has barred my way with blocks of stone;
> he has made my paths crooked.

Yet later in the passage there is hope:

> The LORD is good to those whose hope is in him,
> to the one who seeks him;

it is good to wait quietly
for the salvation of the LORD.
It is good for a man to bear the yoke
while he is young.

Let him sit alone in silence,
for the LORD has laid it on him.
Let him bury his face in the dust—
there may yet be hope.
Let him offer his cheek to one who would strike him,
and let him be filled with disgrace.

For men are not cast off
by the Lord forever.
Though he brings grief, he will show compassion,
so great is his unfailing love.
For he does not willingly bring affliction
or grief to the children of men.

To crush underfoot
all prisoners in the land,
to deny a man his rights
before the Most High,
to deprive a man of justice—
would not the Lord see such things?

Who can speak and have it happen
if the Lord has not decreed it?
Is it not from the mouth of the Most High
that both calamities and good things come?
Why should the living man complain
when punished for his sins?

Let us examine our ways and test them,
and let us return to the LORD.
Let us lift up our hearts and our hands

to God in heaven, and say:
"We have sinned and rebelled
and you have not forgiven.

"You have covered yourself with anger and pursued us;
you have slain without pity.
You have covered yourself with a cloud
so that no prayer can get through.
You have made us scum and refuse
among the nations.

"All our enemies have opened their mouths
wide against us.
We have suffered terror and pitfalls,
ruin and destruction."
Streams of tears flow from my eyes
because my people are destroyed.

My eyes will flow unceasingly,
without relief,
until the LORD looks down
from heaven and sees.
What I see brings grief to my soul
because of all the women of my city.

Those who were my enemies without cause
hunted me like a bird.
They tried to end my life in a pit
and threw stones at me;
the waters closed over my head,
and I thought I was about to perish.

I called on your name, O LORD,
from the depths of the pit.
You heard my plea: "Do not close your ears
to my cry for relief."

You came near when I called you,
and you said, "Do not fear."

He has literally walled Dallas in at times. And I know that
we have both sometimes felt this year that He has shut out our
prayers. I'm convinced, more and more, that what we need
is to sit and wait on Him in silence. I'm convinced that we
need to examine our ways and test them. I want, more than
anything, to claim His promises in this passage—that He will
show compassion and that His unfailing love is indeed great.
I want Him to come near when we call Him, and I want Him
to tell us not to fear.

I need to pray more. Lord, give me wisdom, and Lord,
protect my friend.

---

*To dwell on the past simply causes failure in the pres-
ent. While you are sitting down and bemoaning the
past and regretting all the things you have not done,
you are crippling yourself and preventing yourself from
working in the present. Is that Christianity? Of course
it is not.*

—D. Martyn Lloyd-Jones, *Spiritual Depression*

Dallas is sitting in my office and we both smell like grease.
We've spent a freezing cold afternoon in the garage, where
the car now starts and purrs like the proverbial kitten, with
one push of the shiny silver push-button starter. This after
much tweaking and re-tweaking of the carburetor. We also
put the car on jack stands for the first time, which was nerve-
wracking. "My dad had a car fall on him once," Dallas said

matter-of-factly as we were jacking up the Triumph. "And my uncle got crushed by a camper." Nice.

But getting the car on the jack stands allowed us to see that the clutch leak truly is the result of a faulty slave cylinder.[2] Replace that part, and we'll be driving. Clicking around online reveals that parts suppliers are plentiful, but unfortunately the parts themselves are expensive. For example, we pounded a piece of trim onto the trunk this afternoon that probably amounts to eight inches of metal. Cost: $68 for one piece (two are required—thankfully ours came with the car). "If you ever get short of cash, you can just start unloading trim off your Triumph," Dallas says, half-kidding.

Dallas looks as rough as I've seen him in a long time. His drama with the girl has resulted in insomnia, loss of appetite, and the return of ulcers that have torn up his stomach. "The other night was the first time I seriously considered going to get some coke,"[3] he says matter-of-factly.

"Why didn't you?" I ask. My heart is pounding at the thought of him being that close to getting high. Truth be told, I've lived in fear of this news since we met.

"I thought it through and realized it wouldn't help matters any," he says, not looking up from the table. This is perhaps the understatement of the year. "I think that's what's different about now," he says. "Now I think things through. I was pretty impulsive before." I am around 80 percent convinced that he didn't get high the other night.

2. Full disclosure: I still don't really know what this is, or what it does. I just know that mine is leaking, and that when it leaks it means there's no hydraulic pressure in the clutch, which means that I can't put the car in gear, which means that I can't drive it.

3. Dallas says this so matter-of-factly that it seems like for him, getting cocaine is like the rest of us driving to the corner store for a gallon of milk and a loaf of bread. Weird.

"How are you doing spiritually?" I ask, already kind of knowing the answer.

"I feel kind of dead that way, honestly," he says. His voice is flat and tired and indeed dead-sounding. "I feel like when I pray I'm just talking to myself . . . like it's not doing anything."

I hear myself telling him that how we deal with stress and extreme pressure is, in and of itself, an act of worship. That the act of praying and trusting God is a daily discipline even if things don't necessarily "feel" different. I hear myself telling him that I felt the same way in Ukraine when we were adopting our second child . . . that I actually felt like God was cursing me . . . that He put me on the earth for the express purpose of crushing me to pieces and killing my dreams.

"That's exactly how I feel," Dallas says.

I tell him that I had forgotten all of the answered prayers, all of the blessings, and all of the trials that God had already walked us through. "It's important to actively and intentionally remember those things and thank God for them," I say, remembering all that God has brought Dallas through in the last eighteen months. "He started a good work in you, and He'll see it through to completion."

Kristin and the boys enter the garage with a couple of presents for Dallas. Maxim, my four-year-old, is spastic with excitement. He gets this way whenever anyone opens a present. His excitement brings a smile to Dallas's face. Dallas begins to gently peel back the paper on the package, and he smiles broadly at the gift—a French-press coffeepot. He loves coffee. He opens the other package, which is a parcel of gourmet coffee from an upscale market here in town.

"This is the only present I got this Christmas," he says. He smiles again.

———

Misery loves company
What happened to love
what happened to hate
has change come too late?
The taste of your skin
Was my favorite sin
Living in regret
Of the mistakes that have been
I loved too much
I've learned from my mistakes
Caring at all was too high stakes
Missing you let the hurt begin
Only the beginning of my fulfillment of sin. . . . . . .
                                          —*Dallas*

After some events that have happened in my life lately, I have begun to question my standing with God. I have had to face some hard areas concerning where the dedication of my heart lies. Lately I have felt that I've been letting God down in certain areas of my life, and I realize that my heart has been divided. I have let things come into my life that have hindered my walk with God, and it has had such an impact on me that I've had to evaluate not only my current relationship with God, but my future relationship as His servant. I know that when Christ died, His blood covered not only past sins but the sins that God knew we would commit in the future. That being said, it doesn't make me feel any less guilty for my actions. I have sought out forgiveness in prayer and genuinely have a repentant heart, but I know that things need to continue to change before I will have any peace concerning my walk with God. I know that I need to have more of a heart after God, so the purpose of this essay is to show my thoughts on what that means and how I plan to regain that true heart condition we all should desire as children of God.

If we are to understand what it means to have a heart after God, we should look to biblical examples. The best example we could possibly consider is the life of David. David, through all of his adversity and struggles, turned to God for counsel and protection. David was not perfect, but he strived to serve God as best he could. He stood up in the face of danger and persecution to fight for what he knew to be right in the name of God. What made David a man after God's own heart? It was David's submission to the will of God and his reverential awe of God. David made his decisions based on what he knew to be right in the eyes of God. He had boldness to do the right thing because he was walking with God; therefore, he knew that God was guiding him and protecting him.

So after reflecting on the life of David, how can we learn from him and apply the decisions he made to the decisions we are forced to make in our own lives? We have to look at what motivated David. He saw the holiness of God and the love that God has for His people. You can see this, as well as the love that David has for God, in the book of Psalms. He made God his rock and his foundation. This is what we need to do as well. We need to be God-centered and build our lives upon His foundation. This is how you gain a heart after God—by making Him the center of your life.

We also need to seek after God through prayer, asking Him to soften our hearts and make us the man/woman God wants us to be. We need to evaluate our lives and find the areas that are hindering our relationship with God. The next step we would have to make would be to mortify the sinful areas we have allowed in our lives, and then replace them with things that glorify God.

If we fail to replace those areas, we leave a void that could be filled by things worse than we removed in the first place.

I would like to share what I believe to be the definition of "having a heart after God." I found it in Psalm 1:1–3, which says, "Blessed is the man that walketh[4] not in the counsel of the ungodly, nor standeth in the way of sinners, nor sitteth in the seat of the scornful. But his delight is in the law of the LORD, and in his law doth he meditate day and night. And he shall be like a tree planted by the rivers of water, that bringeth forth his fruit in his season; his leaf shall not wither, and whatsoever he doeth he shall prosper" (KJV). If you look at this description of what happens to people who have a heart after God, why would you not strive to make your heart more God-centered?

In order to truly have a heart for God, we need to submit ourselves to His authority over our lives. We need to seek out His counsel and will for our lives and strive to fulfill that will. Reading His Word and communing with God in prayer are critical aspects of having a God-centered heart. Without true communion and a passion to know God, it would be impossible to have a heart that pleases Him and seeks after Him. So learn who God is, find out what He wants for your life, and think about what He has already done for you. If you do these things, your heart will be easily molded by God to be who He wants you to be.

We need to constantly remind ourselves that the purpose of this life is not to fulfill the urges we have but to glorify God in our actions. Our heart condition greatly influences the way we behave. If we become careless about what our hearts are yearning for, then we put ourselves in a position that leaves us open to all manner of unrighteousness and accusations. Do yourself a favor and evaluate what your heart is yearning for. If your heart is

4. Dallas is using the King Jimmy. See: fundamentalist Bible school.

not dedicated to Christ alone, then make the necessary changes that will bring you back into good standing with God, rather than making decisions you will regret and that will taint your relationship with Him. As always, to God be the glory for what He has done and what He continues to do in our lives. Amen.

8

The Unbearable Lightness of Being an Idiot

I do not understand what I do. For what I want to do I do not do, but what I hate I do.

—Romans 7:15

"My grace is sufficient for you, for my power is made perfect in weakness." Therefore I will boast all the more gladly about my weakness, so that Christ's power may rest on me.

—2 Corinthians 12:9

I hung out with two of my favorite people this weekend— my buddy Zach and a new rock-star friend named Ronnie.[1] One of the things that came up was the fact that he often referred to his good friends—the people with whom he had

1. Front man of an outfit called Joy Electric.

the most fun, laughs, etc.—as "idiots." He said it as a term of endearment, and that was obvious. For example, on Sunday when we were driving to church together, I was trying to describe a good buddy of mine. My new rock-star buddy said, "He's an idiot, like us!" Exactly.

Friends, let me describe why being an idiot is important. First, it means that you're fun to be with because you don't take yourself too seriously and are not afraid to laugh at yourself. This is crucial. It means that when someone gives you a compliment, you just say thanks or, better yet, you make some wisecrack about it rather than saying, "It's only by His good Grace and in Him that I was ever able to even think about writing a book, because I'm a miserable wretched sinner and I want all the attention to go to the cross." For example.

Being an idiot means that while you work hard, you don't take your work too seriously. It means that you're not always on the lookout to "network" or "politic" or "synergize" your way to the top by making sanctimonious, suck-uppy comments to people who can help you get there. It means that you'd rather hang out with people who are fun than people who can move your career forward.

It means that you generally let unimportant things roll off and that you don't sweat the small stuff. It means that you're cool with occasionally telling a story in which you're not the hero and laughing at yourself and even the subculture that you hold nearest and dearest. You probably don't sign all of your correspondence with "Soli Deo ___," or "In Him," or "Grace and Peace." It's just an email, man. It means that you like the movie *Swingers*—this is a nonnegotiable. It means that you like Brad Atchison.[2] It means that you might have read a book or two by Gut Check Press.

My dad is an idiot. My business partner is an idiot. All of my best friends are idiots. We need more idiots in the church, and I need more idiots in my life.

I mention this because of how fun it is to have Dallas back in the house. He is spending the last few days of his Christmas break here, and we're enjoying ourselves tremendously, just being idiots—watching football, listening to music, laughing, and relaxing. He is as relaxed and focused as I've seen him in a long time. His blog posts convey a sense of spiritual growth and maturity.

The trouble comes one evening when Dallas leaves the house around seven-thirty to "go into town." He's been here for a few days and is twenty-two years old, so I don't think much of this. However, his Facebook status says something about the "amazing night he's having," so I follow up via text and find out that he's at a bar, that he's only had "a beer and some nachos," but that he's been chatting up the barmaid all night. The hours melt away, and before long it's midnight and I'm about to go to bed. (Read: Stay up and worry until Dallas gets home.)

```
Hey Bro,
    As I type this you're at Bonnies[3] . . . a
scenario that I'm cool with . . . and we just
texted, which put me at ease some.
    I do trust you, and I respect you as a man
and as a thinker. And this is me probably
```

2. Brad is a big, bearded electric-guitar playing idiot in my church who is a blast to be around.

3. This is a bar in town.

121

over-communicating again, but I feel like I
need to impart some old Christian guy thoughts.

First, I have no problem with bars and occasional moderate drinking. I do both myself . . . you've seen me at Frank's[4] with
Benny, etc. But here's the other thing: There's
really nothing to be gained from a met-a-hot-
barmaid-and-chatted-her-up-all-night scenario,
for a Christian guy. Again, I'm no stranger to
this kind of scenario in which you say to yourself, "She's fun to talk to," and then, "I bet
she'd be fun to make out with," and before you
know it you're in a sleep-deprived, hellish
downward spiral of stress like the one you've
been in for the last month.

I realize I sound like an old, worried lady
right now, but I care about you, man, and I
care about how far you've come. And I know
how easy it is to potentially blow it on some
broad[5] at a bar. I'm confident that you won't do
that. And I'm not a legalist . . . but just remember who you are, in Christ.

Your Brother,

Ted

Dallas arrives at one-fifteen in the morning and we chat
briefly for a minute before I say, "Go get some sleep, and we'll
talk in the morning." I want him to get some sleep because I

---

4. A local sports bar where I sometimes go to watch games with friends.
5. I know this sounds horrible, but we're guys, and sometimes this is how we
talk. I know, on paper, that this girl has value and significance—she has parents,
hopes and dreams, etc.—but in this scenario, the one in which she's unwittingly
undoing all of the good that has taken place in my friend, she's not so special to me.

know he has an important early morning meeting with Mark Criss (from the rescue mission) to talk about him working there this summer.

It's 9:00 a.m. now, and Dallas is still asleep. I've agonized over whether to wake him up or maybe call Mark to smooth it over for him. I've done neither. I think the best course of action is to make Dallas deal with this consequence. I'm just concerned with this pattern of him getting an opportunity and then screwing it up. (As it turns out, he woke up early, called Mark, and then fell back asleep.)

The upside to all this is that I spent a lot of time praying this morning, because I feel pretty helpless, which is good in a "connecting with God" sense. I pray for Dallas, and then I pray for my wife and my own kids, because sitting in my office with the light on at 1:00 a.m. waiting for someone I love to come home gave me a pretty startling vision of what my life will look like in about a decade.

In other news, during my night of insomnia, I successfully ordered a drastically discounted slave cylinder for the clutch, for the almost ridiculously low price of $39.95. I win. Sort of.

If you had told me that I would spend the majority of my day today trying to remove a gunked-up oil filter from the engine block of the Triumph, I would have balked. For whatever reason, whoever had the Triumph before was bent on attaching the filter so tightly that no two stronger-than-average human beings could wrench it off.

We tried the following: an oil filter wrench (fail); jamming a screwdriver through the filter casing and then twisting (major fail, resulting in twisted casing); a pair of huge channel lock pliers (mega fail). Finally, in a fit of rage, I used the pliers to rip the casing off completely, exposing just the base of the filter, at which point we took a hammer and an augur and tried to hammer the thing off. Miserable fail. Freezing and discouraged, we trudged inside. I called my car friend Gary to discuss worst-case scenarios. The words *acetylene torch* entered the conversation. "But of course you don't want to set fire to the engine block," Gary said, stating the obvious. I really hope it doesn't come to this.

***

This morning I do what all good car guys do and bury my head in the proverbial sand, trying my best to forget about the fact that I have a car sitting in my garage that is absolutely no good to me if we can't un-gunk that part in a jiffy. I actually woke up in the middle of the night, worrying about it, among other things. I lay in bed and spent most of the rest of the night praying . . . for my boys, who I feel have gotten the short end of the time-stick since Dallas has been around; for my career, which always seems sort of tenuous; for Dallas; and finally that the filter would come off.

In the morning I decide to get some educational therapy and accompany my second-grader, Tristan, to his classroom, where I know I'll be given a list of menial but super-relaxing tasks like cutting construction paper and gluing things. Below is a list of random thoughts and things that happened between 8:30 and 11 this morning in second grade.

- Whatever Tristan's teacher, Mrs. Sampson, is getting paid, they should double it. She's amazing . . . so organized and in control. I have always respected what teachers do, but this confirms it.

- Mrs. Sampson let me cut a lot of construction paper into strips, which was really fun and, as anticipated, therapeutic. You'll find that many of your problems and issues fade into the background when you're cutting up colored sheets of construction paper. It makes a really satisfying sound too. A lot of people spend a lot of money on counseling, but I wonder if much of this could be avoided by cutting up construction paper?

- I had a kid (Raven) ask me, completely unironically, the following question: "Are you an author and illustrator, or just an author?"

- His disappointed response, upon learning that I'm just an author: "Oh."

- I learned, from a girl named Sarah, that Alistair's fly has been down "like, all morning." (giggles)

- I like that "public school" smell, which is a combination of the following: paper, school lunch, carpet, and industrial-grade cleaning agents.

- I played tag with half the school at recess, and it was awesome.

- This was the most fun I've had in a long time.

Much like the children, I am rejuvenated after recess. I come home and walk right past the car and into my office, not ready to face failure again. I'm realizing that if I put it out of my mind and just avoid walking by it, it ceases to exist. I hear Dallas's work boots clomping through my hallway.

"Ted, where you at?" he asks. I brace myself for a tough conversation of some kind. Instead, he comes into my office in his Carhartt jacket, holding the mangled remains of the old filter. "I taught it about authority," he says triumphantly. I grab my jacket and dash into the garage, rejuvenated.

"I took the hammer and chisel and just pounded on it," says Dallas, holding the mangled shard of oil filter triumphantly.

Within minutes we have the new Fram filter installed (correctly, this time) and a five-quart jug of clean, honey-like motor oil *glug-glugging* into the engine. We seal it up, crank the car down from the jack stands, and fire it up. It seems to run even smoother and idle even lower (good) than before. We're one step closer to driving.

Tonight I celebrate our car progress with a movie night out at a friend's house. When Kristin and I return around midnight, we find Dallas pacing and smoking in front of the house. I can tell from his voice and mannerisms that I'm going to be up for a while talking with him. I'm beyond exhausted, but it's also very clear to me that this conversation is the whole reason for Dallas being here—more than the car, and more than just giving him a place to relax.

In a nutshell, he is despondent because of the temptation he's feeling, sexually.

"I feel like a womanizing (expletive)," he says. "I've completely turned into my father."

I've noticed that, almost nonstop since he arrived, Dallas's cell has been vibrating, chirping, and spitting out songs. The phone is Dallas's conduit to woman drama. This is the kind of drama that results in stress-filled, semi-sleepless nights like this one, but it's also the kind of drama that young, single people live for. I know that it gives Dallas's life meaning, to some degree, to know that he can be attractive to women, and it gives their lives meaning to know that they can attract Dallas.

"I use women," he says. "It's been this way for as long as I can remember. I lost my virginity when I was ten years old. I remember every single thing about the experience. And since then, until I became a believer, sex was pretty much a daily part of my life. I'm a dirty guy."

"Dallas, we're all dirty guys," I tell him. I rub my temples and try not to dwell on how utterly heartbreaking it is that Dallas was just two years older than my Tristan when he lost his virginity. Dallas is describing a struggle for purity that has happened, at some level, to every Christian guy who has ever walked the face of the earth.

Dallas is an interesting study in contrasts. He is very protective of the women in his life and gets very angry when women are disrespected. "I gave a guy a harelip in a bar once," he says. "I was in the bathroom and came out, and this guy had his hands all over my girl. I started smashing his face against the cigarette machine. . . . They had to take him out in an ambulance."

He is pacing around my office, agonizing over an invitation he's received to go to Ann Arbor, where a hotel room and a girl from his old life are waiting for him.

"She's amazing, bro," he says. "She's got a perfect body, she's beautiful, and the best part is that we connect intellectually. We talk for hours . . . she's a talented writer, she's interesting . . . she's perfect. I've been after this girl for the past six years."

But she's not a believer. "Dallas, you can't go," I tell him. "In no way can you go down there. I'm not your father, and I have no authority over you, but as your friend, I can't let you go. I'll wrestle you to the ground and break your ankle before I let you go down there."

He smiles a little bit for the first time since we started talking. He shows me a picture of the girl. She has glasses and one of those trashy-hot lip rings. It's the kind of lip ring that communicates something along the lines of "If you buy me a drink or five, I'll probably sleep with you." This isn't an indictment of the girl, it's just what the lip ring communicates. It is semi-hot. Dang.

"If you go down there, Dallas, a lot of things will be different. You'll no longer be battling sin but willingly engaging in something that you know is wrong. It brings the Book into question. . . . It brings a lot of things into question."

"I know, bro," he says, "but it's so hard. It's so hard to flee temptation. What I want to do I don't do, and what I don't want to do, I do."

These words, from Paul's letter to the Romans, pretty much accurately summarize the heartbreaking struggle with sin. But it is this struggle that casts the hope of the cross in an even more glorious light. Without an acknowledgment that sin exists and is real and is in our hearts, the cross is rendered meaningless. I quote the father of the boy with the evil spirit from Mark 9:24, as I pray for Dallas: "I believe. Help my unbelief."

When he wasn't texting, checking his cell, writing on Facebook, or otherwise flirting with girls, Dallas spent much of the day in Scripture and in prayer. I'm glad. The rest of the day he spent at the Mission, where he feels utilized and at home. He preached to the homeless guys again at lunch.

"I love the Mission so much, bro. I feel like it's home. But I feel like such a sham," he says, "preaching to them, but then dealing with this."

I let him know that he's not a sham, but that the decisions that he makes over the next twenty-four hours are critical. I encourage him to turn off his phone and the computer. To basically go dark. "Bro, you don't owe these girls anything," I tell him. "You're not raising their kids, you're not paying their bills . . . you're THEIR entertainment, just like you're using them for yours."

"I just want what you and Kristin have," he tells me. "I want the white picket fence . . . I want a girl I can talk to and grow old with. I want a Christian girl."

"Well, if you keep chasing barmaids, and especially if you drive to Ann Arbor to hook up with Lip Ring, you can kind of forget about that (Christian girls). . . . You're going to scare them to death. A girl like Kristin won't want anything to do with you. A Christian girl will forgive your past—she'll forgive the pre-conversion Dallas—but she's not going to put up with what you're thinking about doing now."

He tells me that he drank a little tonight. "I went out and bought a half-pint."

I look at him. Dead air.

"I'm so sorry, man," he says, his eyes misting over. "I'm so sorry I let you down."

"You didn't let me down, bro," I tell him. "It's just that, I dunno, I worry, you know? You're a recovering substance abuser, and you're my friend. But Christ died for this; He died to cover worse than this."

Now he's sitting in my office, crying with his head in his hands. We pray.

129

"Lord, your Word says that your power is made perfect in our weakness, and, Father, I pray that Dallas and I would feel that tonight. Lord, we're both weak. We're both tired. We're both tempted. Lord, give Dallas strength, give him wisdom, and help him to feel your forgiveness and grace. Your Word says that if we confess our sins, you're faithful and just to forgive us and cleanse us of all unrighteousness."

I look up and Dallas is sobbing. Tears are streaming down the black sleeves of his leather jacket. He does have boyish good looks. It occurs to me, for the first time, that he looks like the Matt Dillon character in *The Outsiders*, who was named Dallas and had a very similar life to my Dallas.

"Every time anybody prays for me like that I cry," he says.

"Bro, I'm thirty-four years old, and anytime my mom prays with me like that, I cry like a little girl." I hug Dallas and tell him I love him. The next twenty-four hours are going to be critical.

9

Trying to Kill Sin,
Because Right Now It's Killing Me

*Do you mortify; do you make it your daily work; be
always at it whilst you live; cease not a day from this
work; be killing sin or it will be killing you.*

—John Owen, *The Mortification of Sin*

*An unmortified lust will drink up the spirit and all the
vigour of the soul, and weaken it for all duties.*

—John Owen

Dallas wakes up the next morning (and by morning, I mean
noon), and has begun to pack up and load his truck. "I'm
heading down to see Marcus for a couple of days," he says.

"How far is Marcus from Lip Ring?" I ask.

"A ways."

I help him load his things, and it occurs to me that all of
Dallas's earthly possessions are represented here, in a few trips

up the stairs from the basement. There are baskets of clothes, some personal care items, laundry detergent, a couple pairs of shoes, and a leather jacket. He looks exhausted and on the verge of tears. I know that he slept for only a couple of hours the previous night. Anxiety and temptation are eating away at him.

In the particular sub-subculture that we are a part of (Young Reformed-dom), it's cool to dig puritans. This is something I never thought I'd see, yet for the Young Reformed Christian, a book isn't any good unless it was either written by a puritan guy who's been dead for a few hundred years, or a current guy writing about a puritan guy[1] who's been dead for a few hundred years. Either way, Dallas and I aren't puritans. We're seedy guys. We're the kind of guys who smoke cigars and laugh at lowbrow movies.[2]

But it occurs to me this morning that I need to take a more active role in helping Dallas kill sin. And Owen's quote about actively killing sin before it kills you is especially real to me today. I am releasing Dallas back out into the battle. We embrace, and I tell Dallas that I will be praying for him. "And I'm going to nag you a bunch too."

He smiles. My kids race to the door to give him a hug. They love Dallas, and I know that their innocent, childlike, naïve love has a profound impact on him. For the balance of the day and into the next morning, I pray short little prayers in my head, like "Lord, be with Dallas" or "Lord, help him fight temptation."

1. Reading some of these guys is like watching paint dry, although as a young, Reformed person, it's important to act like you love all of them.
2. We sat on my sofa and watched *Beavis and Butthead Do America* the other night and howled through the whole thing. I'm pretty sure if Jonathan Edwards were alive today, he wouldn't have joined us (but Spurgeon might have . . . especially if we were smoking). It makes me sheepish to admit in print to liking this movie.

I also periodically send him texts just to see how he's doing. John Owen writes, "Sin will not only be striving, acting, rebelling, troubling, disquieting; but if let alone, if not continually mortified, it will bring forth great, cursed, scandalous, soul-destroying sins." He continues, "There is no safety against it but in a constant warfare."

This warfare imagery is something that Dallas and I can relate to. He's been in more fights than he can remember, and as a football player and boxer, I've been in my fair share as well. We can both relate to the idea that if you're not winning, you're losing. I have temptations as well—to frustration, jealousy, anger, discontentment, sarcasm, and self-pity—and helping Dallas to mortify his sins is good practice for me too.

One that I've always struggled with is cynicism. I like protecting my heart from pain. When I watch a movie that I know is going to be sad, I want to figure out which character is going to die first, so that I can begin to emotionally distance myself from him. Cynicism dulls our emotions and kills our ability to dream and hope. Paul Miller, author of *A Praying Life,* has this to say about cynicism: "Shattered optimism sets us up for the fall into defeated weariness and, eventually, cynicism. You'd think it would leave us just less optimistic, but as humans we don't do neutral well. We go from seeing the bright side of everything to seeing the dark side of everything. We feel betrayed by life."[3]

I think Dallas feels betrayed by life. Truth be told, I do too sometimes. I spent the morning wallowing in self-pity, reading press releases about an NFL quarterback with whom I was going to do a book but who signed to do it with someone else. By the end of the morning I was entertaining fantasies

---

3. Colorado Springs: NavPress, 2009.

of seeing him hauled off on a stretcher with a broken neck. I'm a horrible person. Cynicism, according to Miller, sees "a dark cloud in every silver lining." True story.

I worry about the same things Dallas is worrying about— the inability to pay bills, an uncertain future, etc.—except on a slightly larger scale. I'm reminded of a Mark Driscoll sermon on Philippians 4, in which he explains that "Anxiety is a sin to be repented of, not a condition to be managed." I try my hardest to repent of it. But these days, in the winter in Michigan, I look out the window every morning, see new snow falling, and just want to crawl back into bed.

Unable to pray effectively this morning, I remember an exercise in Miller's book, in which he was describing an especially painful point in his life. It was so painful, in fact, that he couldn't manage to read his Bible or pray. Rather, he just prayed through the Twenty-third Psalm each morning, over and over. I begin to do the same thing . . . thinking of myself, and Dallas, as I read:

> The LORD is my shepherd, I shall not be in want.
>   He makes me lie down in green pastures,
> he leads me beside quiet waters,
>   he restores my soul.
> He guides me in paths of righteousness
>   for his name's sake.
> Even though I walk
>   through the valley of the shadow of death,
> I will fear no evil,
>   for you are with me;
> your rod and your staff,
>   they comfort me.
>
> You prepare a table before me
>   in the presence of my enemies.

You anoint my head with oil;
   my cup overflows.
Surely goodness and love will follow me
   all the days of my life,
and I will dwell in the house of the LORD
   forever.

I pray that the Lord would lead us beside quiet waters—
that He would quell the drama in Dallas's life. I pray that He
would continually be restoring our souls, even as we walk
through the valley of the shadow of death. I pray that our
cup would overflow . . . that Dallas and I can know what
it feels like to occasionally not have to worry about money.
And I do pray that goodness and love would follow us all
the days of our lives—that Dallas would be surrounded by
good, humble, kind, solid people who love him and care
for him.

I then turn my attention to Psalm 25, specifically a verse
that I had underlined two years before while I was suffering
in Ukraine—sick, cold, tired, and broke—while adopting our
second child. Verses 16–17 read: "Turn to me and be gracious
to me, for I am lonely and afflicted. The troubles of my heart
have multiplied; free me from my anguish." Anyone who has
ever despaired, or who has ever been addicted, can feel the
weight of those words in a personal way.

———

Dallas calls briefly and I learn three things. The first and
most important is that of his own volition, he went into
the office of the administrator he'd had a run-in with and
apologized to him for the way things unfolded the previous
semester. "I just felt like a jerk for how I handled that, and

how I lost control of my emotions," he tells me. "That wasn't me, and not how I want to be."

I am so proud of him for this, as it's evidence of a sensitive conscience and a teachable heart. I also know that this gesture will go a long way toward building some goodwill in the coming semester.

I also learn that the girl who was involved in most of the drama during first semester, and who was expelled over it, will be returning to school in the spring. The drama basically consisted of Dallas and this girl insisting on being together— (talking, texting, eating meals together, going on dates, etc.)— which is all pretty normal stuff except that it took place at a school where that sort of thing (dating) is against the rules.

Relations between the two of them, thus far, have been chilly, but they're both functioning fairly well, independently of one another. Her presence will ratchet up Dallas's anxiety level at school and make the semester significantly less smooth, but I assure him that he's up to the task and will be able to handle it. "Keep your head down, bro," I tell him. "Just do your work, be kind to her, and handle things in a classy way."

Finally, I learn that he loves his French-press coffee maker. He takes it to class with him each morning; it has become something of a fixture by his side. "People are bringing me special coffee beans for it, man," he says excitedly. This makes me smile.

It's 8:00 p.m. and I've already heard from Dallas three times today. He called at seven-thirty as I was driving into school and once in the afternoon when he was out looking for jobs, so when I saw his name on the phone a few minutes ago, I let it go to voicemail. My wife had purchased a bottle of wine, brought home sushi, and lit a candle. If you're a married guy and you're reading this, you know exactly what this means: It's on. The fact that It's On means that I can't spend half the evening on the phone with Dallas. I can smell my wife's perfume, which is faintly raspberry-ish and super sexy.[4] Ahh. The phone rings again.

I look at her and she looks at me. This is something of a moment of truth. It's a moment that says, "You're really good at making all of your friends feel loved and affirmed, partly because you're willing to listen to their calls and talk to them at all hours of the day/night, but you need to let this one go." I envision Dallas sitting outside a crack house or in a ditch somewhere. I press the talk button.

"Hey, bro, I just need to talk about something . . ." He launches into a story about how he once had a drink with a student who had been expelled, and on his way out, the student had told someone in the administration about the drink with Dallas. "I only had one, bro, and I just wanted to let you know . . . I don't want to disappoint you or jeopardize anything."

I tell Dallas to relax and that his conduct thus far this semester—his willingness to humbly apologize—will have built some goodwill with the powers that be. I tell him to low-key it, and that it will probably blow over. I tell him (again) that I trust him in the area of alcohol, but to be careful. I tell him that I love him and hang up the phone.

Upside: Dallas and I talk briefly about an idea I've been mulling over: for Dallas to ink me up[5] upon completion of the

4. I bought it for her for just such moments as these.
5. Meaning to tattoo me. If you're reading this and you're my parents, feel free to put the book down now and flip out.

car/book. He is super excited about this and has been in the process of mocking up designs and locating tattoo equipment.

Downside: Kristin is reading a book, the candle has been extinguished, and the moment, unfortunately for me, has passed. I'm again reminded (the hard way) that discipleship is more than a bi-weekly cup of coffee.

"The call to discipleship . . . means both death and life . . . [It] sets the Christian in the middle of the daily arena against sin and the devil. Every day he encounters new temptations, and every day he must suffer anew for Jesus Christ's sake. The wounds and scars he receives in the fray are living tokens of this participation in the cross of his Lord."

—Dietrich Bonhoeffer, *The Cost of Discipleship*[6]

Maxim, my four-year-old, is so cute this morning. He crawls into bed with me and, instead of jumping on my stomach, he just lays next to me (we share a pillow) and sucks his thumb and alternately dozes off/stares at me. It is so nice. I love that kid so much. It's been weird this year . . . at times I've felt so focused on Dallas that I sometimes forget I have my own kids who love me and need me. The phone vibrates.

Dallas texts and says, "Bro, I think they're turning me into a fundie!"[7] Okay, I'll bite. He calls a second later from

6. Touchstone, 1995, 99.
7. It's about time I define this. Fundie, loosely applied, means fundamentalist Christian, which on paper means a lot of things that I agree with, like the inspiration of Scripture and Christ's death and resurrection as the only means for salvation. George Marsden famously wrote that "fundamentalists are evangelicals who are angry about something." The best definition I found came from http://www.stufffundieslike.com and is as follows: "For these posts, 'fundamentalism' means

his bunk, where he's been laid up with the flu for the past several days. "I've been reading this book, man, and it's really opening my eyes about Calvinism." He says that he's been grappling with Scripture, Calvin's *Institutes,* and this book for days. I assure him that my goal in life isn't to make him a card-carrying Calvinist.

"And I had a conversation with (girl)," he says. I let the sentence hang in the air for a moment. Here we go. "I gave her a devotional book by Spurgeon and told her that we both need to focus on our spiritual lives this semester. She agreed." I can hear peace in his voice for the first time in a long time.

The peace gives way to turmoil a few days later, however, when Dallas is told that his grandfather is bleeding internally and that the bleeding can't be stopped. "I'm driving down to Ann Arbor tonight to be with him," he says. I also learn that the school isn't allowing Dallas to visit AA (Alcoholics Anonymous) meetings while he's living on campus, stating that "they're not biblical." This news, almost more than any other, makes me want to put my fist through a wall. They have no idea what recovering addicts need, which (in part) is accountability and a chance to be around people who understand what they're going through. I make a note to follow up on this with the Mission and with someone from the school.

AA was founded in 1935 and now has over two million members. It is a program of spiritual and character development founded on the Twelve Steps and is credited with helping

'Independent Baptist Fundamentalism,' a movement that rejected not only liberal theology but also those parts of the culture that it considered to be 'worldly' such as certain types of music, styles of dress, the theater, alcohol, and many others. These fundamentalist churches also separated themselves from association with any other movement they deemed too liberal or worldly; in fact, separating from things soon became their greatest distinctive—and a source of amusement to those of us who grew up in the movement."

many alcoholics in their battle for sobriety. It certainly isn't a total "fix," but it's a place where Dallas can be around like-minded men who have the same struggles and the same need for accountability.

While there are certainly theological bones to be picked[8] with the Twelve Steps approach, I think in general the idea that we're powerless in the face of sin (in this case alcohol abuse), and that we desperately need to turn our lives over to the care of God is a pretty good place to start. The Twelve Steps include admitting to God, and to another human being, the exact nature of our wrongs. Again, this seems biblical, as is the idea of humbly asking God to remove our shortcomings and trying to make amends with the people we've wronged.

Dallas has been involved with groups like this on and off since he began to work on his sobriety in the Lansing area. One of his favorites was Celebrate Recovery, a program that started in 1991 at Rick Warren's Saddleback Church. The CR program stresses that there is no higher power except for Jesus, and it is available as a sort of Twelve Step program for all manner of addictions and hang-ups, rather than limiting itself to alcohol. CR also unpacks the Twelve Steps to include Scripture references for each, to give members a theological understanding of their recovery journey. Although opinions are mixed on Warren and Saddleback, I find this approach incredibly helpful.

For example, in addition to admitting that we are powerless and our lives have become unmanageable in Step One, CR adds Romans 7:18, which reads, "I know that nothing

8. Namely the idea that AA allows its members to choose their own "Higher Power," suggesting that there are higher powers equal to that of the one true God as revealed in Scripture. To be fair, this is a pretty major theological bone. However, I still wish Dallas could go to AA once in a while.

good lives in me, that is, in my sinful nature. For I have the desire to do what is good, but I cannot carry it out." And in Step Seven, "Humbly asking Him to remove our shortcomings," CR adds one of Scripture's most comforting promises, from 1 John 1:9: "If we confess our sins, he is faithful and just and will forgive us our sins and purify us from all unrighteousness."

Warren also devised a list of Eight Recovery Principles based on the Beatitudes:

1. Realize I'm not God; I admit that I am powerless to control my tendency to do the wrong thing and my life is unmanageable. "Happy are those who know they are spiritually poor."
2. Earnestly believe that God exists, that I matter to Him, and that He has the power to help me recover. "Happy are those who mourn, for they shall be comforted."
3. Consciously choose to commit all my life and will to Christ's care and control. "Happy are the meek."
4. Openly examine and confess my faults to God, to myself, and to someone I trust. "Happy are the pure in heart."
5. Voluntarily submit to every change God wants to make in my life, and humbly ask Him to remove my character defects. "Happy are those whose greatest desire is to do what God requires."
6. Evaluate all my relationships; offer forgiveness to those who have hurt me and make amends for harm I've done to others except when to do so would harm them or others. "Happy are the merciful"; "Happy are the peacemakers."

7. Reserve a daily time with God for self examination, Bible readings, and prayer in order to know God and His will for my life and to gain the power to follow His will.

8. Yield myself to God to be used to bring this Good News to others, both by my example and by my words. "Happy are those who are persecuted because they do what God requires."

In reading the list, I'm struck anew by the repeated mention of the word *happy*. There should be some joy present in our lives and relationships, even in the midst of tough circumstances. Is my greatest desire to do what God requires? I pray for happiness for both Dallas and me, in our individual lives and in our relationship with each other.

Tonight, though, Dallas is despondent. He is trapped in Ann Arbor by a broken rear axle. "I drove too fast over some train tracks," he says. I am tempted to say something like, "Do me a favor and just limit your comings and goings to your classrooms, your dormitory, and the cafeteria, because when you leave campus in your truck, bad things tend to happen to you." I don't say this, but I seriously consider it. Unfortunately, he catches me on a day when I am equally despondent and the world seems black. Our funds have run out, and I don't have the money to float Dallas for a new axle or anything else at the moment. I am tapped out, financially and emotionally. Lord, help us.

In his book on prayer, Paul Miller explains that "He wants us to lose all confidence in ourselves because 'apart from [Jesus] we can do nothing;' he wants us to have complete confidence in him because 'whoever abides in me and

I in him, he it is that bears much fruit (John 15:5)."[9] I am
struggling with losing all confidence in myself, because that
idea flies in the face of the American ethics of self-suffi-
ciency, swagger, and independence. We are literally down
to our last few hundred dollars and are waiting on some
advance checks that as per publishing industry standard
are glacial in arriving. Paul (not Miller, the real Paul) says
in Romans 8:26 that "The spirit helps us in our weakness.
We do not know what we ought to pray for, but the Spirit
himself intercedes for us with groans that words cannot
express."

Every day Dallas is trapped in Ann Arbor is another day
the car isn't getting done. The slave cylinder has sat in a box
in my office for weeks, and I haven't even opened it. The part
itself is insultingly small . . . and the fact that this is the only
thing keeping me from driving feels like a slap in the face.

"I might go to work with my brother tonight . . . try to
raise up some funds to get out of here," he says.

It will be three days before I hear from him again. I get a
call from the administrator at the school, but because of Dallas's three-day silence, I don't have anything to report to him.

Meanwhile, the greater Lansing area is battening down
its proverbial hatches in preparation for what is being billed
as the snowstorm of the century. There are huge crowds at
grocery stores, as people have been encouraged to stay inside
for days to ride out the storm. The snow begins to fall around
midnight, and I can hear the wind lashing the side of my
house. The storm, and Dallas's financial hardships, give me

9. Miller, *A Praying Life.*

little hope that we'll be able to unite this weekend to work on the slave cylinder.

When a slave cylinder goes bad, it basically means that the seals inside the clutch have gotten worn out and the clutch has begun to leak fluid, meaning that one day you depress the pedal to shift, and instead of pressure in the clutch bouncing it back up, it stays on the floor of the car, and you're unable to put the car into gear. An awkward, grating, grinding sound ensues.

We'll need to jack up the left front side of the car and remove the wheel, and the slave cylinder should be visible just inside the wheel well. We'll also need to bleed all of the old fluid out of the clutch and run new fluid through it so that there are no air bubbles in the line.

I hear from Dallas, via text today, that he is still in Ann Arbor and that his grandfather was released from the hospital. Nobody knows exactly what caused his internal bleeding, but it has stopped and he seems to be out of the woods for now. As a result of the snowstorm, Dallas has picked up some snow removal work and will hopefully be able to generate the funds needed to fix his truck and get back up to school (via my house). I sleep well, thankful that God is answering some of our prayers in tangible ways.

10

Give Light to My Eyes or I Will Sleep in Death

*But I trust in your unfailing love; my heart rejoices in
   your salvation.
I will sing to the LORD, for he has been good to me.*
                                                —Psalm 13:5–6

Dallas is down for a weekend visit, and the slave cylinder
project is turning out to be much more than we've bar-
gained for. As it turns out, it's more beneficial to get at the
cylinder through the cockpit of the car, so we first remove the
driver's side seat, under which we find the following:

- A grocery list written on a sheet of paper from Im-
  manuel Reformed Church in Grand Rapids, suggesting
  that perhaps a Calvinist owned the car previously. I don't
  know why this makes me feel better, but it does.

- A sheet of Burger King coupons from 1990.
- A large piece of cowling that must be removed if we're to get to the part we need.

We begin the herculean task of unscrewing this vital part of the cockpit, and gain a whole new appreciation for how close we are to the road when we see the garage floor through the frame of the car after it is removed. Once it's gone, we can access the slave cylinder, which is a three-inch part. All this trouble for three inches.

As soon as we access it, we realize why the clutch hasn't been working. It's completely shot and eroded, inside and out. The previous owner had been using the wrong kind of brake fluid (DOT 3 as opposed to DOT 4, and no, I don't know what this means), which ate away at all of the rubber bushings in the slave cylinder . . . resulting in an eroded, leaky mess.

Aside: We decide to listen to old British pop (The Rolling Stones) while we're working on an old British vehicle. I like this cohesiveness very much. We even take a break for tea and cookies. Seriously, we do.

It seems like everything on this car has seized up. We have to spray magic de-gunker on all of the nuts and bolts and then let them sit. It's been said that working on an old car is like taking an old person to the doctor . . . once you get them in there, you start finding all kinds of things that are wrong.

Fast-forward three hours. With the cockpit in pieces on my garage floor, we are at a standstill. The brake line on the Triumph won't be coerced into the new slave cylinder, which itself took some coercing (read: pounding with a rubber mallet) to get into place. This isn't helped by the fact that a) it's freezing outside, and b) there are about two inches of space in which to work and turn the wrench. Dallas and I are both big guys, so it's difficult for us to squeeze ourselves underneath the steering wheel to access the slave. Once underneath the dash, we can turn the wrench only about a half an inch each time, so progress is slow and painstaking.

Finally, we try to muscle the brake line into place, though neither of us feel good about this and fear that we've cross-threaded the new slave. We forge ahead with the next step, which is "bleeding" the clutch, meaning that we run some new (correct) fluid through the system to eliminate air bubbles. Because of my enthusiasm for the Paul Miller book on prayer, I've been muttering more frequent, smaller prayers in my head. I'm silently praying that this part works so that Dallas and I can feel some success.

It doesn't. When we run the new fluid through the system, it squirts out into the bleed pan under the car. We take out the slave and try one last resort, flipping it over and re-threading it. Same result. Leaky brake line. Epic fail. Apparently we bought a junky new part from Victoria British, whose name invokes images of guys sitting around sipping tea with their pinkies out, reading Henry James novels. Now I'm sure this isn't the case.

There's a whole subculture, I'm learning, that is crafted around these classic British cars and their enthusiasts. I become a small part of this subculture by subscribing to *Classic Motorsports* magazine. *Classic Motorsports* caters, from what I ascertain from their ads and articles, to guys in their mid-fifties with lots of time and money to dump into ridiculously cool classic cars from Europe that they then spend

what's remaining of their time/money taking to rallies, pho-
tographing, and showing off to one another. This scenario is
not unattractive, but it does seem a long way from the hunk
of metal currently resting in my garage. Hence the glut of
parts-supplier ads in the back of the magazine from whom
you can buy every part you could conceivably need to build
one of these things from scratch in your basement.

Victoria British is located in Lenexa, Kansas, and is probably not a quaint British cottage operation, but rather a depressing warehouse in a depressing strip mall. I'm depressed
because now they have my fifty bucks and I have a completely
useless part that I can't return.

I start to get the frantic, angry, dejected feeling that I've
gotten every time I've ever played a sporting event and lost.
I feel defeated, ironically, by the Triumph. The name on the
back bumper mocks me. The car feels more like an adversary,[1]
or something to be beaten, than a friend. I see a red door and
I want to paint it black.[2]

The day, however, isn't a total loss. "We still accomplished
a lot today, bro," Dallas explains, sensing my dejectedness.
"The part I thought was going to be hard—getting the inside
of the car apart to get to the slave—was easy, and the part I
thought was going to be easy (reattaching the brake line), was
hard. That's just the way it goes working on cars sometimes."

It's strange, this feeling of putting in an entire day's work
and having nothing to show for it. As a writer, when I write

1. Oddly, I've begun having dreams at night of completing and driving the
Triumph . . . feeling its knurled wood-grain stick shift in my hand, gliding smoothly
through all four speeds. Wind whipping through hair. That sort of thing. I do this
(the dreaming) every time I've ever undertaken a handyman-ish project at which
I have no confidence and perhaps even no hope of completing (see also: my deck,
completed; the boxing ring in my basement, also completed).
2. Rolling Stones.

for two hours I at least have several pages of work in front of me. In this case, we've worked for eight hours and have nothing to show for it except a messy garage and a partially disassembled car. However, we did have a great day of conversation in which I learned:

- Dallas has been running an underground "store" out of the closet in his dorm room, but instead of selling narcotics, he's selling Gatorade and snacks to students who want good food but don't want to go off campus to get it. "The administration shut me down," he says, "but I still operate with a sign that says 'Donations Welcome.'" Given Dallas's size and appearance, I'm sure donations aren't just welcome—they're expected.

- Dallas has been encouraged by answered prayers lately. "When my grandpa went to the hospital, they didn't know the cause of the internal bleeding, and they didn't know how or if they were going to be able to get it stopped. But they were able to stop the bleeding, and he's home now." This news encourages me tremendously.

Right now I'm relying on Dallas to encourage me, as he seems more optimistic than I do.

If you read my last post, you could easily tell that I have been struggling with some things recently. It has taken a while for me to realize what the sources of those struggles were and face them head on. After a lot of thought, prayer, and action, I feel like a new man. I am once again invigorated about my spiritual walk with God. I have eliminated the things in my life that were sucking the joy out of me. I have a fresh new perspective. I want to share this with you readers to inspire hope, because even in the darkest times God is still good, and He will see you through whatever problems you may be facing.

Attitude is key. Try to remain focused on being the best person you can be and, more important, having the best relationship with God you can possibly have. Always remember that the circumstances of the past are exactly that. THE PAST! Even if those circumstances happened yesterday or earlier today, it's still . . . you guessed it: THE PAST! Try to release all regret and worries, because there isn't much you can do to change it anyway. All you can do is look forward to the future and enjoy today for the beautiful blessing it is. God is sovereign, He is in control, and He will always bring about the better good, even if we can't see it clearly because of the storm surrounding us. Find comfort in the fact that He has a holy plan for our lives.

As important as attitude may be in dealing with your problems and mistakes, it is only part of the solution. You must take action! First, you need to take action in prayer, laying these issues at the feet of our Lord and then listening to the wisdom He gives through His word. Second, once you have done this, you must heed His advice and take action in your own life to correct the problems you're facing. This may seem hard in the moment, but ultimately it is liberating. Rid yourself of people or things that have been dragging you down, then break the chain attaching you to them. They can act as an anchor dragging you into an abyss of astonishing depths. Don't let yourself be taken on a ride that you don't want to be on.

Again, it's about attitude. In order to take the action required to bring about change, you have to humble yourself and be willing to accept that things don't always turn out the way you want them to. We are here to bring about God's will, not our own. A little humility goes a long way when dealing with the problems we face in life. More often than not, trials are put in our paths to stretch us and help us grow stronger. You have to remain optimistic and never accept defeat. The only person that can bring about defeat in your life is yourself, by giving up. So show the world what a true soldier of Christ looks like by becoming the definition of perseverance and strength. By standing strong in the face of tribulation, God will be glorified; it shows the faith that you have in Him to guide you and hold you up when all you feel like doing is lying down and accepting defeat.

Stand strong, my Christian brothers and sisters, because this too shall pass. While we're facing trials, time can seem to slow to a stop, but you must remember that it is only temporary. Look forward to the brighter day of tomorrow, and try to find contentment and joy in today while learning from your circumstances. The Serenity Prayer has taken on such beauty and truth to me lately; I hope it transforms your perspective as it has mine. God grant me the serenity to accept the things I cannot change, courage to change the things I can, and the wisdom to know the difference, amen. All glory to the only One who deserves it: God.

—————

This week I heard from one of my former football players at Williamston High School, where I coached defensive line for two seasons. This particular player was one of my favorites because he showed up for the first day of practice with long hair and a vintage *Miami Vice* T-shirt.[3] I immediately began calling him Sonny Crockett, but his nickname morphed into Jackie Moon when I learned that his first name was Jack.

Defensive line is sort of the Ellis Island of high school football inasmuch as we get everyone else's castoffs. Players

3. T-shirt day two: I (heart) New York.

who weren't athletic or cooperative enough to contribute in other places were funneled to me on the defensive line. While other coaches had players who wore Michigan Football Camp Under Armour T-shirts and Midwestern tough-guy crew cuts, I had Jackie Moon.

One of the things I appreciated most about Jackie Moon, who I knew had gotten into some trouble off the field, was his aversion to what I would call "typical" coach-rah-rah-talk. Simply put, even though he was way too small for defensive line at five-feet-eight and about 160 pounds, I figured at the very least he could entertain me each day and break the monotony of practice. He did so splendidly. He also ended up being my starting nose tackle, because in addition to wielding a razor-sharp sarcastic sense of humor and an appreciation for movies and travel,[4] he had an incredible willingness to do absolutely everything he was told and endure huge amounts of punishment, which is pretty much the nose tackle's lot in life. A glamour position it's not.

But being a starting player on a playoff team afforded Jackie Moon, for the first time, a bit of social caché that had previously eluded him, meaning that he got to wear a letterman's jacket and he became popular. Jackie Moon secured his starting job a few weeks into the season and never let it go, save for a suspension for an off-the-field issue late in the season that, truth be told, kinda broke my heart. After his last game—our playoff loss—we embraced on the field and sobbed like chicks because, truth be told (again), the end of a football career is pretty much one of the hardest things a

4. Our defensive line drill sessions, between drills when everyone was bent over panting and sucking down water, were like mini-cultural seminars for Jackie Moon and myself. I daresay it's this kind of thing that I miss most about football.

young guy has to endure. Football is so *finite*. Once it's over, it's *really* over, never to be heard from again.

Jackie Moon was my favorite player even though coaches aren't supposed to have favorite players.

Fast-forward two years. I receive a Facebook message from him to the effect of: "Life has gotten really hard, there's no joy for me in anything, sometimes I cry for no reason and I have no idea what I'm going to do with myself."[5] Besides perfectly describing my own mood much of the time, it gives us an excuse to sit down over burritos two days later and talk about how Christianity is the only religion that isn't about what you can do for God, but about what God did for us through Christ's atonement for our sins on the cross. I tell Jackie Moon that this atonement, and the hope for eternity it provides, is my only real comfort on this earth and my only shot at true joy. Not money. Not prestige. Not my family. Not my books. Not even the ridiculous, second-only-to-sex kind of pleasure I got from playing competitive football. "And the things that I've been able to achieve and enjoy in this life, as I look back and reflect, are gifts given to me by the Lord, including football, my family, and my work…. Not to take this discussion in a super-spiritual direction or anything," I add sarcastically.

Jackie, to his credit, asks the tough questions, just as I knew he would. The fact that he is the kind of kid who asks the tough questions probably has a lot to do with the fact that he's also the kind of kid who, even though his every material need is provided for, finds himself wildly unhappy. "You being

5. Difficult reality check: My wife says to me shortly thereafter, "I feel like every sad and confused young male in the greater Lansing area sometimes gets more access to you than I do." My response, after apologizing and meaning it, was, "But this is why I coached football—for conversations like this."

dissatisfied is, in a way, proof that you're created in God's image but living in a fallen world," I tell him. And then he asks me what may be the mother of all tough questions: "If God is truly God, why does He need me to worship Him? It seems like He's asking for an awful lot."

I would be a liar if I told Jackie Moon anything other than the fact that I've pondered that very thing myself. "It's not so much God needing our praise and worship," I tell him. "It's that by fully recognizing the problem of the human heart—that is our sinfulness and total depravity—we can come to understand that glorious gift of grace that Christ gave us on the cross." Jackie, like most truly thoughtful people (including, for what it's worth, Mike Tyson), really gets this intuitively and doesn't have to be told that the human heart is wicked. But I would argue that really getting this is the first and maybe most important part of really understanding the gospel in all its fullness. It's what makes Christianity something you're willing to die for, rather than just an exercise in religiosity. It's the understanding of our own fallenness and then Christ's redemption that motivates us to praise, thank, worship, and fix our eyes upon Jesus, the author and perfecter of our faith. I even went so far as to do something I hardly ever do, which is to suggest that maybe the very fact that we were sitting down over burritos was evidence that the Holy Spirit himself may have been doing some work in the heart of one Jackie Moon. We agree to meet again.

I receive the following text from Dallas: "Hey, bro, could you do me a favor and pray for me? I need some strength and wisdom."

Me: "Will do. What's happening?"

Dallas: "Thanks, bro. Just trying to make some wise choices with (girl). Just making the best decisions for our future. I told her we need to talk tonight because I see some of the same patterns developing as last semester, and I'm trying to stop things before they get out of hand."

Me: "Be her leader in that, both in terms of the attitude stuff and the physical stuff."

He calls a little later to tell me that he has "left campus for a few minutes" so that he doesn't "break somebody in half." The somebody, I learn, is his girlfriend's ex-boyfriend, who has shown up on campus on Valentine's Day, unannounced, bearing flowers and a new dress for her. I can tell that Dallas would like nothing more than an excuse to cave this guy's face in, and it sounds like to some degree he deserves it. But Dallas is already on probation for aggravated assault, and a fight with this guy would probably get him a one-way ticket back to lockup. I gently remind him of this. "I know, man. I just feel so disrespected," he says, voicing perhaps the number one reason sober guys get into fights at all. For a man there is perhaps no worse feeling on earth than the feeling of being disrespected. I can hear the despair in my friend's voice, but I tell him that I'm glad I'm hearing his voice right now. I'm glad he called me instead of waiting around on campus to rearrange some guy's face.

"I've been doing really well this semester, man . . . I even stopped smoking before today," he says. He tells me that he scraped together his remaining change just to be able to buy a cigar and a flower for the girl. "I'm going to write her a letter and just tell her how I feel . . . how hard this is for me," he says.

155

We pray together that he would be wise and prudent and that the love of Christ would be evident in him. And I even give him a few words to say, should he and the ex-boyfriend happen to cross paths. "Tell him it will be in both of your best interests to not talk right now," I say. "He'll know what you mean."

Dallas is having his best week yet at school. He's in the midst of working a week-long camp for youth pastors and is soaking up "twelve hours of preaching a day," and then spending his free time setting up the auditorium for speakers.

He's hearing great preaching and becoming reinvigorated and re-motivated for the ministry he'll be doing in the summer for the Mission. And what's more, he's having "more fun with fundies than I ever thought possible." Those are his words. Mark that down as one of the things I never thought I'd hear him say. Because he's not spending all of his time talking with his girlfriend about how terrible school is, he's actually meeting and enjoying other students and finding out that the place isn't nearly as terrible as he thought it was.

It occurs to me that while sin always divides (see: Old Testament, Israel, the judges, etc.), it almost always, initially, seems to unite. There is an intense feeling of camaraderie in mutual rebellion against a place, leader, idea, rule, etc. I can only imagine the thrill that Dallas and his girlfriend must have felt, sneaking off campus to talk about how much they disliked the school and how ridiculous the rules were, and to engage in the breaking of those rules. Actually, I don't have to imagine it. I experienced it at my own Christian college where there was a very real and intensely loyal community of kids who united in hating the place.

I feel like God has been stripping Dallas and me of our rebellious spirits this year. This morning in Hebrews I re-read the quintessential text on Christian discipline, which helps to shape our theology of hardship and suffering. I think it speaks to the kinds of trials that Dallas and Jackie Moon have undergone this year, as well as the kinds of things I have struggled with (failed adoption, book deals, etc.).

> "My son, do not make light of the Lord's discipline,
> and do not lose heart when he rebukes you,
> because the Lord disciplines the one he loves,
> and he chastens everyone he accepts as his son."

Endure hardship as discipline; God is treating you as sons. For what children are not disciplined by their father? If you are not disciplined (and everyone undergoes discipline), then you are illegitimate children and not true sons. Moreover, we have all had human fathers who disciplined us and we respected them for it. How much more should we submit to the Father of our spirits and live! Our fathers disciplined us for a little while as they thought best; but God disciplines us for our good, that we may share in his holiness. Later on, however, it produces a harvest of righteousness and peace for those who have been trained by it. (Hebrews 12:5–11)

A few things occur to me for the first time as I read this passage. One, Dallas barely had a human father who disciplined him and to whom he could give respect for it, which must make it doubly hard for Dallas to swallow the heavenly Father imagery we see so much in Scripture. Second, how hard it is to truly submit to the Father of spirits because of how much we cling to our besetting sins—our attitudes, the conditions of our heart, and for me, the occasional attitude that God created me just so He could beat me up. This is as wrong and sinful as wrong and sinful can be, and I ask forgiveness for it. And finally, I'm struck by how hard it is to wrap my head around the idea of a harvest of righteousness and peace. I have a difficult time imagining peace for a day, much less a harvest of it . . . yet I want that desperately, both for myself and for Dallas.

And it's this—the righteousness and peace harvest—that makes the suffering anything but meaningless or, worse, arbitrarily mean. Our trials are proof of our legitimacy as sons and daughters of God.

In *The Everlasting Righteousness,* Horatius[6] Bonar[7] writes: "There are degrees of rest for the soul, and it is in proportion as we comprehend the perfection of the work on Calvary that our rest will increase. There are depths of peace which we have not yet sounded, for it is 'peace which passeth all understanding;' and into these depths the Holy Spirit leads us, not in some miraculous way, or by some mere exertion of power, but by revealing to us more and more of that work, in the first knowledge of which our peace began."[8] The cross, according to Bonar, accomplished three things: 1) The death of the old man; 2) the destruction of the body of sin; and 3) deliverance from the life-bondage of sin.

At dinner I share this quote with my wife . . . the idea that peace and joy is somehow found in the unceasing, repeated comprehension of the cross. "I would love to do that," I tell

6. There's nothing Reformed people love more than a good old-dead-guy reference.
7. Giggle.
8. Jefferson: Trinity Foundation, 1994.

her, "but the truth is I spend most of my time not thinking about the cross." What's weird is that the particular subculture I'm in, church-wise, is great at talking about the cross all the time—that is, putting it in book subtitles and scoring hypothetical conversational points with it. . . . But I'm not sure simply understanding it and then talking about it is enough.

It is my hope and my prayer that both Dallas and I will feel and experience this in a real way. Knowledge is one thing, but true heart-level submission is another thing entirely.

It's the beginning of a new semester here at school, and things have been pretty amazing. I have approached things in a different manner this semester, coming back with a fresh perspective on accomplishing my goals, and it has really paid off. Last semester my personal biases made me critical of everything here, but I should have been trying to make my time here profitable. I let my pride hinder the work of the Holy Spirit in my life, and once that happens, the problems only escalate. Fortunately God is very patient, and He extended his grace by opening my eyes to these facts and humbling me.

Now that I have a fresh perspective on things and a renewed humility, I have had more fun than I thought possible with a group of fundamental Baptists. We just spent the last week hosting a youth pastors' conference that was life-changing for me. We had twelve solid hours of preaching every day, reinforcing my passion to reach people with the Gospel. There is such a great need to work with young people and help them before the world robs them of their innocence. The call to disciple and defend the youth from the evils of this world is ringing out! Who is going to have the courage to answer that call? We need to commit ourselves to encourage these kids, because they are the future of the faith we hold so dear.

Dallas and the Spitfire

People are constantly asking why the body of Christ has taken the turn that it has, why people are less willing to hold to biblical truth and more likely to adopt worldliness. The answer is this: There is a lack of godly influence in the lives of young people, as there are not enough people willing to dedicate their time to helping mold young Christians into the godly men and women they need to become. As Christians, we are commanded to build others up in the faith, yet the majority of us are perfectly content to just fill a pew on Sunday and consider our Christian duty fulfilled! That is not living life for God.

There are ministry opportunities right in front of our faces every day, but the average Christian walks blindly along, ignoring the opportunity to be a blessing. God through His sovereignty has placed people in our lives for a reason. When you face God at the time of judgment, will He say to you, "Well done good and faithful servant"? Are you being a good steward of all that God has entrusted you with, including the well-being of the souls around you? These are the type of questions that have changed my perspective and my walk with God. Are you willing to honestly examine your daily walk with God and ask these questions of yourself?

Kids are facing hard issues like sex and drugs at earlier and earlier ages. It is so critical for us to be a part of their lives so they have somebody to turn to when they face these things. If we are called to a life of love and service, how is it that so many Christians stand idly by while kids are making decisions that will destroy their lives? As you read this, I hope the call to defend our youth rings loudly in your ears. These kids need your help. Will you have the courage to stand up and be the godly man or woman that our Lord has ordained you to be? Will you be that good and faithful servant, or will you stand by as our youth make decisions that will hinder their relationships with God and alter the future of the church?

I call my dad tonight because I need to be discipled. I'm the one who feels dejected, defeated, and like putting my fist through a wall (or someone's face). A book project proposal I have been working on with yet another crazy athlete[9] has fallen through, seemingly without explanation or reason. I am depressed beyond words and questioning my existence as a writer and as a provider for my family.

My dad, true to form, is calm and reassuring. He doesn't quote Scripture during my call, but instead tells me that he's spent the whole afternoon online reading things that I've written and reading about me. That means more than just about anything he could have said, because it communicates loyalty. I long for, more than almost anything else, people's loyalty, as I know that Christ demands absolute loyalty from me.

"That project falling through probably saved you a huge headache in terms of working with that guy," he says. "It might be for the best." He tells me that he's in the process of re-reading my first book. I thank God for him.

Dallas is struggling too. I get the following email from him, which I've included exactly how it was received, typos and all, because I feel like they (the typos) sort of add to the desperation of the whole thing:

9. See a pattern developing here? No more dealings with ridiculous famous former athletes. When I say "crazy athlete" in this context, it means someone who never reads or writes, yet wants to "write" a book in which on each of the two hundred pages they look like a hero or do something amazing. This is why there are so many bad sports biographies out there.

Hey bro,

I really appreciate all the help you and everybody at URC have given to me in the past i hate to ask but I'm starting to really struggle financially and i could really use your help. I'm trying to find work and haven't came up with anything so far. It's been a real test of faith lately because I'm flat broke and have bills coming from everywhere it seems like and no means to pay them. The mission took care of the remainder of the school bill but they aren't able to help out with my living expenses at all now. Hopefully God blesses me soon because I'm in pretty bad shape with my truck being out of commission, no way to file for an extension on my taxes, and bills piling up, and to top it all off i have a mission trip that i have to go on to graduate and no way to pay for it. It seems like everything is going to pieces lately even my shoes lol. Anyway man if you could help me send this letter out I would really appreciate it, i sent it in an attachment its just a letter describing the trip and the purpose of it.

Here's the attached fund-raising letter:

Dear _____,

I am excited about this rewarding year[10] that the Lord has given to me at (school name omitted). He has blessed me in so many ways already!

10. Nobody talks like this in real life. Especially Dallas. And while he would describe the year in many different ways, many of them even positive, I don't know that he would ever use the phrase "rewarding year."

162

On April 29, (school name omitted) will be taking a missions trip to New York and Chicago for 9 days. Some of the students will be going to New York and some of the students will be going to Chicago.

We will have the opportunity to go soul-winning,[11] run children's programs in the parks, and show people how they can have hope through Christ. The men will be preaching in the subways, and the women will be sharing their testimonies, along with other opportunities.

What an awesome privilege! I thank God for what He is allowing each of us to do. I trust Him for His power to accomplish His purpose through our lives during the missions trip.

I desperately need people to pray for me during this Missions trip. What we will be doing the Devil[12] does not like. There will be battles with the world, the flesh, and the Devil. As part of the team, you can commit to pray for us on a regular basis.

We have taken this challenge of faith to raise our financial support. The support goal has been set at $600.00. If individuals and/ or churches could each give something, we will exceed our goal. This is a real step of faith for us. Please pray about becoming a part of the financial Support Team. I will be very grateful!

11. Dallas would never say this either, because he knows he's not the one "winning the souls."

12. It's interesting how we create the "character" of the devil (horns, pitchfork) in letters like this. Sometimes I think we give him too much power with statements like this. God, after all, is sovereign.

Our theme verse for LiveRight Baptist Bible Institute is, "As ye have therefore received Christ Jesus the Lord, so walk ye in him," Colossians 2:6. With God's help and much prayer, hundreds will be saved and students will continue to commit their lives to full-time service. Thank you for your interest in me and our preparation for the Lord's service.

I ask you to join us in the ministry as we seek your support and prayers for this mission trip. Thank you in advance for your prayers and your financial support. May God bless you richly!

Love in Christ,

Dallas Jahncke

It occurs to me how cheesy and insincere and "institutional" the fund-raising letter sounds when compared with the authenticity of his email. I know this isn't his fault, as the fund-raising letter smacks of something boilerplate-ish that the school probably put together for them, which means it sounds like every boilerplate fund-raising letter ever written by every lapel-pin-wearing, meaty-fingered development guy in the evangelical world. Sending out stuff like this is basically a rite of passage for Christian college students, but I just hate these things because of how contrived they all sound. The school would have been better off just letting Dallas write his own thing.

The fact is, we've got a hunk of metal in the garage that needs our attention. And if we can get Dallas through the last few weeks of school in one piece, financially and otherwise, he's got a great job with the Mission waiting for him when he gets out. And we'll both get a much-needed infusion of cash when we turn the manuscript in.

It is at some point in Peeter Lukas's garage (temperature, a nippy 37 degrees Fahrenheit) that I really understand the nature of discipleship. Peeter is fifty-four and has the most memorable of handlebar mustaches. He has a degree in library science (or something) and works on the line at General Motors. He has been doing this, basically, forever. And he requested a GM transfer to the Lansing, Michigan, area[13] so that he could go to the church that we both go to. He's an elder there. The church is the reason we're in the garage today. Actually, the reason we're in the garage as opposed to the house is the fact that we're smoking cigars. He did the church-lobby thing and asked how I was doing, and I think I groaned or rolled my eyes or something. Peeter is that rare cat with whom I totally don't BS in the church lobby. I'm fake and "surfacey" with nearly everyone else I encounter there, so much so that I'm sure this admission will come as no surprise to anyone. I hate the church lobby like I hate few places on earth. Like a root canal, it's something to be gotten through.

Other awesome, random things about Peeter:

- He has a completely functional several-thousand-book library in his basement that includes actual Dewey-decimaled stacks of books. I know because I helped move the books there. There are also a bunch of sweet empty

13. Nobody moves here of their own volition—seriously—except Peeter. The winters alone are godforsaken, like we've been sentenced to Siberia. And it gets worse the farther north one goes in Michigan.

bottles and album covers and other stuff framed all over the place. It's the kind of basement I could happily spend days in.

- He used to have a 1978 Triumph Spitfire the same color blue as ours, and told me that buying it was the "stupidest thing" he ever did. The fact that he would tell me that in light of his knowing about this project is actually very refreshing. Usually people just tell me whatever I want to hear, and believe it or not this sometimes gets old.

Peeter wears two coats while he smokes. He smokes good cigars, not the cheap drugstore stuff that is the dead giveaway of a cigar poseur. He always lights with matches. The garage is full of old-guy stuff like tools, a vice of some kind, and garden implements. "Sometimes I just sit here and smoke and look at the deer walking past the back door," he says. I nod, wishing like crazy I was the kind of guy who could be satisfied sitting and looking at deer walking by the door. Someday.

I talk and we smoke. I talk about the pain of infertility. I talk about the grind of being a professional writer and how burned out I am on the "hustle," and how it's not even that, like, *exciting,* or whatever, to see the books in print because I'm always so fixated on getting the next deal because I'm always out of money. We talk about how hard family life can be at this age and how interminable and somewhat unsatisfying and joyless the whole thing (life) seems sometimes. I tell him that I could probably be capable of some serious self-destructing, all morals aside. He empathizes and tells me about some of the serious self-destructing he did as a young man, and how he still sometimes has long stretches where he doesn't sleep more than a few hours a night. I tell him that 2:30 a.m. is my new "morning," and that three to four hours seems to be commonplace for me now, and not because I'm one of those gifted "high energy" people who can work, like, twenty-one hours a day and then crash for three hours on a cot and be fine. I'm not. I'm in the midst of a serious career crisis and am re-evaluating whether I even want to keep writing. I'm working on a book that seems to be sucking the life out of me (not this one, the football-player one).

Before he prays for me, Peeter gives me a book on grief by C. S. Lewis called *A Grief Observed*. "Don't read the rest of his stuff on grief," he says. "It's all theological gobbledygook." It warms my heart that he's willing to say this about Lewis. I've always secretly thought it. Lewis is one of those authors you have to pretend you love if you're a Christian. But I can tell after reading a page and a half of this book that it's going to blow my mind and speak to me exactly where I'm at. Lewis wrote it, not intending for it to be published, after his wife died. It's a book about being angry and confused about God and then ultimately sticking with your faith. It's exactly what I need.

Then he prays for me.

———

Dallas calls today with the news that his truck has officially breathed its last. "I think the electrical system is totally shot," he says. He walks me through a long explanation that includes the words *starter* and *solenoid* and *tried everything*, and then ends with, "Yeah, I think it's shot. I'm not sure I can make it down." This makes this week's logistics especially difficult, because this is when he's supposed to come down and help me finish the car. In fact, this is the week photographers from the publishing company are showing up to take our pictures with the car.

What's hard is that whenever anything like this happens, I get the call and feel like I'm expected to come up with something. Tonight, though, I can offer nothing besides, "Bro, you *have* to get down here. It's not optional. This is a work thing." That being said, I still hash together an email that will go out to the church, asking if anyone has a vehicle lying around that they can donate to the Dallas cause for a few months, to get him through until he can buy another one. We then begin cobbling together a plan to get him down here that includes bus schedules and potential rides with friends.

I feel pretty gored-out, spiritually and logistically. Like, an "I have nothing more to give" kind of feeling. The week to come, which for me includes teaching my college classes, taping four episodes of a new radio show[14] I'm involved in, and getting the parts for and fixing up the Triumph, feels like it's going to be nearly impossible to pull off. Our family is also, incidentally, nearing its own personal financial rock bottom. Before bed I pray the following: "Lord, forgive us for the ways we've failed. Forgive us for the poor decisions we've made. But Lord, *please* give us some tangible signs of encouragement tomorrow that we can clearly see are sent from you."

The Lord provides the following tangible answers to prayer the next day: Mark Criss, from the Lansing City Rescue Mission, offers to drive to school to get Dallas and bring him down to Lansing. The Lord also provides some tangible encouragement for me in the form of a potential full-time

14. "The Reformatory." Check us out online at www.remedy.fm.

teaching job that would alleviate some of the pressures of a full-time freelance writing career, for the first time in years offering us some financial stability.

Speaking of stability, I'm getting more and more comfortable going into auto-parts stores and asking for things. Today I'm at the Carquest in Grand Ledge, Michigan, looking for a five-foot piece of 7/16 brake line that we will need to finish installing the slave cylinder. I can tell I'm getting more comfortable in these places because the guys behind the desk banter with me like I'm one of them, instead of getting all stilted and weird, like they get when a woman comes into the shop. Except that the guy looks at me like I'm crazy when I say I need 7/16. "That's a HUGE piece of brake line," he says. "Lemme show you." He walks me over to where they keep the different sections of brake line. "See, 7/16 is like a huge piece of pipe." He's right; it's like the upright on a goal post. "I would bet that you'll need a section of 3/16 line." He shows me that line, and it looks like exactly what we'll be taking out of the Spitfire. I thank him and pay him, and inside I'm thanking him for not making me feel like an idiot.

Back home, the mood in the garage is semi-celebratory. Dallas is here, and he's in great spirits. He's changed his lifestyle a bit and is now going to bed early and getting up early, which has him looking and feeling refreshed. He was up at 6:00 a.m. and in the garage, removing the old brake line and slave cylinder. By the time I shuffled out at seven-thirty in my pajamas, he was well on his way to halfway done, determined to finish the car before the end of the day. What's more, his eyes are clear, he's chatty, and he seems genuinely full of joy. I haven't seen this Dallas in a long time, and I'm glad he's back.

We're joined in the garage by my buddy Gary, who has come to help with the slave cylinder project, and Peter, a photographer from the publishing house, who will be here all day snapping photos, and who takes about five minutes to become one of the guys. Soon he's busting chops[15] and enjoying the "hang" with the rest of us.

The project isn't without its complications. The piece of brake line I bought has the wrong-sized fitting on one end, so we realize we'll have to cut the line (requiring another tool) and then re-flare the end of the line (yet another tool purchase) so that it holds the replacement fitting. It's worth mentioning here that Gary's help is invaluable. He's totally in his element in the garage, and he and Dallas hit it off immediately. "Gary shared some of his testimony with me in the car," Dallas says later. "His life sounds a lot like mine."

As Mark Driscoll sermons play in the background, the car slowly begins to come together. Once the new slave cylinder is in, the big test will be to see if the clutch builds pressure and the car shifts correctly. Dallas slides into the vacated spot where the driver's seat used to be and begins pumping the pedal. "We've got pressure." Huge relief. He then begins taking the transmission through its shift pattern. "Shifts smooth." We high-five and embrace.[16] The pace in the garage becomes a little frantic as we work to put the cockpit back

15. I'm getting my chops busted for being the only guy in the garage who takes sugar in his coffee. Dallas and Gary, of course, take it straight black. The photog just takes a drop of cream, which they've somehow deemed more manly than a little sugar. I tell my wife, "Look, just bring me out a glass of rocks and broken glass and I'll drink that, okay? Is that manly enough for you guys?"

16. Seriously. But then we immediately make a joke about the scene in *Rocky III* where Rocky and Apollo frolic in the surf together, which is without a doubt one of the most embarrassing things ever portrayed onscreen, even though we both love *Rocky III* and all of the *Rocky* movies (except *Rocky V*, which nobody loves).

together so we can fire the car up and drive it. Our frozen fingers work overtime to tighten down the cowling and put the carpets back in place. I stop the room and motion for the photographer with the shifter knob in hand.

"Peter, I want you to get this, man. This is my contribution to the project," I tell him. "Not to take the focus off Dallas, but this is really about me and what I'm going through," I joke as he snaps shots of me screwing the wood-grain shifter into place. Triumphant (pun, please pardon), I slide into the driver's seat with the keys and turn on the ignition. I press the cool-looking silver button. Nothing. This is a bit of an anticlimax, to say the least. The hood goes up and there is more furtive checking of things. We finally determine that this battery—which came with the car and is who-knows-how-old—is deader than the proverbial doornail.

Meanwhile, posed shots are taken. I can tell that this is a way new experience for Dallas, who is being told to put his chin down, but look up, at the photographer. It's weird even for me. He puts us in all manner of supposedly "natural-looking" poses around the car and tells us to banter naturally even though we're standing in ways we'd never stand in real life. I start quoting movie lines, trying to crack everybody up to lighten the mood. "For a relaxing time, make it Suntory time." I say this in my best "Bill Murray in *Lost in Translation*" voice. It breaks the tension a little. There is all kinds of visionary talk about Dallas and me taking a book tour and driving from stop to stop in the Triumph.

I have to leave to broaden minds in a college classroom for three hours, but my mind is on the Triumph. I leave Dallas with my almost-tapped-out plastic and instructions to pick up and install a new battery. When I return, the car is sitting in the garage and ready to go. "Wanna fire it up?" he asks. I grab the keys and almost run out to the garage. I toss him the keys and slide into the passenger's seat for the maiden voyage. He's done the bulk of the work, and he deserves it. I always struggle with moments like this. I don't want to make an awkward speech that ruins the moment by trying to sum it up or capture it in some way. Dallas keys the ignition on, and before hitting the silver button says, "This is so awesome, bro."

"This is the culmination of a lot of hard work," I tell him. "Enjoy it." With that, he hits the button and the engine springs to life. Cue throaty rumble. He's been through a lot this year. Graduating the Mission's rehab program. Surviving school without getting kicked out (praise God). Staying clean and sober (praise God again). Surviving his first real, heartbreaking relationship with a woman, which is a male rite of passage. And most important, growing in his faith in the Lord. I thank God that we've survived it, and even enjoyed it.

We back the car out onto Castleton Drive, and Dallas puts it into gear (smoothly, I might add). It's all of twenty-four degrees outside, but the sun is shining. We aim the car north, and Dallas hits the gas. It springs to life. Carburetors, clutch, brakes, radiator, and engine all working as they should. People look at us like we're insane.

I look over at Dallas in his black leather jacket. He's smiling, and he looks just like James Dean.

Epilogue

Discipleship and Playlists

Why believe the devil instead of believing God? Rise up and realize the truth about yourself—that all the past has gone, and you are one with Christ, and all your sins have been blotted out once and for ever. O let us remember that it is sin to doubt God's Word. It is sin to allow the past, which God has dealt with, to rob us of our joy and our usefulness in the present and in the future.

—D. Martyn Lloyd-Jones, *Spiritual Depression*

I've been driving the car a lot lately. I'll walk into the cold garage, slide into the driver's seat, pump the pedal a couple of times, key on the ignition, and listen to the engine spring to life. Sometimes I'll take my wife for short jaunts around the neighborhood, during which she'll ask cute questions about the car and about cars in general—questions that I now have answers to. Her: "Why is it so bumpy?" Me: "That's how it is in a sports car; it means we're feeling the road.

"Do you want me to punch it a little?" I'll ask as we round the corner from Cotswald Lane onto Castleton Drive. "This is a residential neighborhood," she replies, right before I press the pedal floorward. She smiles. I think of our fourteen years together—especially the last twelve months—and the struggles we've been through. I'm happy we're together and that we're partners in all of it. She sent me a text earlier that said, "I've really been enjoying you lately." This makes *me* smile.

It occurred to Dallas and me toward the end of the project that it would be a shame not to make an iTunes-style playlist of the "soundtrack" of the project—songs that were meaningful to both of us as we worked in the garage and wrote. Some of the songs are British. Some of them are about drugs. Some of them are songs about struggle, and winning and losing. Some of them are just songs we like. They are in no particular order, and some of them are of the "Parental Advisory" persuasion, so use your discretion. Listen while you read, if you want.

1. Johnny Cash, "Cocaine Blues"
2. 50 Cent (featuring Eminem), "Patiently Waiting"
3. Creation, "Making Time"
4. David Bowie, "Life on Mars"
5. Five Finger Death Punch, "The Bleeding"
6. The Who, "Baba O'Reilly"
7. Notorious B.I.G, "Hold Ya Head"
8. The Kinks, "Nothing In This World Can Stop Me Worryin' 'Bout That Girl"
9. Tim McGraw, "Just to See You Smile"

10. The Rolling Stones, "Paint It Black"
11. Rich Mullins, "Awesome God"
12. 30 Seconds to Mars, "This is War"
13. Guns N' Roses, "Night Train"
14. Nico, "These Days"
15. The Doors, "Riders on the Storm"
16. The Clash, "Police and Thieves"
17. Paul Simon, "Me and Julio Down by the Schoolyard"
18. Mark Driscoll, "Philippians: The Rebel's Guide to Joy in Anxiety" (sermon)
19. Mark Driscoll, "Philippians: The Rebel's Guide to Joy in Exhaustion" (sermon)
20. Iggy Pop, "Gimme Danger"
21. Mark Mothersbaugh, "Let Me Tell You About My Boat"

Dallas's truck has again been coerced to life, and he calls to tell me that he wants to come down and visit but doesn't even have the money to fill his gas tank. "And if I did," he says, "I'm not sure how I'd get back." This is a common refrain. Unfortunately, the author is semi-broke at this point as well. "Let's keep trusting God," I tell him. "He's been faithful this whole year. But that said, you probably should have gotten a richer mentor."

"Bro," he says, "I wouldn't trade what we have for the world."

Acknowledgments

From Ted

To my good friend Dallas. I love you, man. None of this—the book, the car—holds a candle to the fact that you're my brother in Christ, and you're like an uncle to my sons. It's a privilege to have a friend like you. Thank you for being my friend, and thank you for bearing with all of the mistakes I made this year. If nothing else, this book is a great chronicle of our friendship, and it will always mean a lot to me.

To my dad, for teaching me absolutely nothing about cars, but teaching me everything about being a hard worker, a devoted husband, and a man of God who also knows how to have a good time. Thanks for always including me in absolutely everything. To my mom, for putting up with both of us and basically being awesome, loving, kind, and giving in every way. I learned the art of giving myself up for others from you.

To my sweet wife, Kristin, for looking like Audrey Hepburn in our convertible. For loving adventure. For not being, in any way, boring. For putting up with me and all of my adventures.

For accepting Dallas into our lives, and for caring for him. For caring for me so well. Here's to a lifetime of adventures, my darling.

To Tristan and Maxim, my sons, for your enthusiasm and for generally making everything I do feel more awesome just by being a part of it. I adore you both. My prayer is that as you grow older, you would both be discipled and disciple others.

To my pastor friends, Zach and Cory, for demonstrating what it's like to be about discipleship without constantly talking about "discipleship."

To my agent, Andrew Wolgemuth, and my editor on this project, Andy McGuire, for being cool in a business that can seem like it doesn't have very many cool people in it. Thanks for believing in this project.

To our URC small group—Dan and Priscilla, Ben and Jami, Matt and Emily, Kevin and Trisha, Nick and Emma, and Nathan—for your support and prayers through this project.

To John Vandenburg from the Bible Institute . . . we didn't always agree on everything, but you were always willing to talk, and I believe that you sincerely care about my friend Dallas. Thank you for taking care of him while he was there.

To Mark Criss, Rich, and everyone else who works so hard to make the Lansing City Rescue Mission what it is—a tough but amazing place for men and women to know the Lord and work on breaking free from their addictions.

To Gary Strpko for not once making me feel stupid for not being able to identify anything about the inside of cars. Thank you for taking me hot-rodding around the back roads of Eaton Rapids, Michigan. For your expertise in cars, and your Wyatt Earp mustache. Thanks also to Libby for the haircuts and for letting me hang out with Gary, encouraging him in his completely impractical car hobby, and not getting too mad about all the junk he has in his garage.

To Zach (again) for helping me run Gut Check Press and for the trip to Bay City to see your father-in-law and his car collection.

To Brad, the previous owner of the Triumph Spitfire. Thanks for not screwing me on the deal, even though you totally could have.

From Dallas

I would like to thank the many people who have had such a huge impact on my life these past couple of years. It would be impossible to mention you all by name, so if I have left you out, it is not out of ungratefulness but for the sake of time— I could nearly fill another book just with names of people who have been a blessing to me. So with this in mind, I will address the people who have made the greatest impression on me by their unwavering compassion, loving me not just as I am but as the man of God they had faith I would become.

The Lansing City Rescue Mission will always be my home and family because of the love shown to me there. I owe a special thanks to Mark Criss, Mike Hayes, Rich Gray, and Brian McGruder for your patient investment in me. You saw me at the lowest of my lows and you refused to give up on me. You dedicated your time, love, and guidance to me when most would have written me off as a lost cause. You tested me and challenged me daily with practical life lessons, which made me a stronger man, capable of fighting the temptations I face every day. Mark, you in particular have been such a great friend and have become like a father to me. You have my most sincere love and respect for showing me your daily walk with God and what it means to be set apart from this world. You have helped mold me into the man I am today, and for that I am deeply indebted to you.

To my family at University Reformed Church, I thank you for the support you have given me while I have been at school, as well as the friendship and brotherly love you have all extended. You have embraced me in your lives, brought me into your families, and have made me feel like I am at home whenever I am fortunate enough to be in your company. Kevin DeYoung and Ben Falconer, you are my pastors, my leaders, and most important, dear friends. I thank you both for the solid teaching and preaching you faithfully put forth every Sunday; it is through this that I have been built up in the knowledge of God, enabling me to begin to live a life that glorifies Him.

To Ted Kluck, my friend, my confidant, and my brother in Christ: I owe you a great deal. Without you, this project would have never come to fruition. You have endured frequent phone calls, hard conversations, and my hard-headedness since you took on the task of mentoring me. You have helped me to see clearly the truth in the word of God when my vision was blurred by the storms of life. You have helped me overcome many obstacles, and you held me up at times when I felt like throwing in the towel. My friendship with you and your family is a precious gift from God that I value beyond measure.

Above all, I thank God for the amazing work He has begun in me. The sacrifice Christ made on the cross to save such a wretched soul as mine is what started the transformation I have been going through. His love and grace has given me a new life, and that is why I lay this life at His feet, eager to serve our Almighty God of compassion. I owe it all to you, Lord. My goal in this book and in my life is to share the amazing work that you continually bring about in me and through me. I thank you, Lord, because I know that what is inscribed on these pages is only the beginning of an eternal relationship with you.

Additional Resources

Addiction/Recovery

Lansing City Rescue Mission: www.lcrm.org
Celebrate Recovery: www.celebraterecovery.com
Alcoholics Anonymous: www.aa.org

Christian Books

Bonar, Horatius. 1994. *The Everlasting Righteousness, or, How Shall Man Be Just with God?* Jefferson: Trinity Foundation.

Bonhoeffer, Dietrich. 1998. *The Cost of Discipleship*. Nashville, Tennessee: Broadman & Holman Publishers.

Bridges, Jerry. 2007. *Respectable Sins*. Colorado Springs: NavPress.

DeYoung, Kevin. 2009. *Just Do Something*. Chicago: Moody Publishers.

Kluck, Ted. 2010. *Hello, I Love You: Adventures in Adoptive Fatherhood*. Chicago: Moody Publishers.

Lloyd-Jones, David Martyn. 1965. *Spiritual Depression: Its Causes and Cure*. Grand Rapids, MI: Eerdmans.

Miller, Paul E. 2009. *A Praying Life: Connecting with God in a Distracting World*. Colorado Springs: NavPress.

Owen, John. 2004. *The Mortification of Sin*. Edinburgh: Banner of Truth Trust.

Ryle, J. C. 2010. *Holiness*. Chicago: Moody Publishers.

Great Sermons

Mark Driscoll: www.marshill.com/media/sermons
John Piper: www.desiringgod.org
University Reformed Church/Kevin DeYoung: www.urc-msu. org

Other Interesting Drug/Addiction-Related Books

Kluck, Ted. 2006. *Facing Tyson: Fifteen Fighters, Fifteen Stories*. London: Lyons Press.

Peter, Jason, and Tony Neill. 2008. *Hero of the Underground: A Memoir*. New York: St. Martin's Press.